CONVERSATION BOOK 2

Pam Tiberia
Janet Battiste
Michael Berman
Linda Butler

Boston, Massachusetts   Burr Ridge, Illinois   Dubuque, Iowa   Madison, Wisconsin
New York, New York   San Francisco, California   St. Louis, Missouri
Bangkok   Bogotá   Caracas   Lisbon   London   Madrid   Mexico City
Milan   New Delhi   Seoul   Singapore   Sydney   Taipei   Toronto

McGraw-Hill

A Division of The McGraw·Hill Companies

CONNECT WITH ENGLISH: CONVERSATION BOOK 2

Copyright © 1998 by the WGBH Educational Foundation and the Corporation for Public Broadcasting. All rights reserved. Printed in the United States of America. Except as permitted under the United States Copyright Act of 1976, no part of this publication may be reproduced or distributed in any form or by any means, or stored in a data base or retrieval system, without the prior written permission of the publisher.

This book is printed on acid-free paper.

domestic 1 2 3 4 5 6 7 8 9 0 QPD QPD 3 2 1 0 9 8
international 1 2 3 4 5 6 7 8 9 QPD QPD 3 2 1 0 9 8

ISBN 0-07-292765-8

Editorial director: Thalia Dorwick
Publisher: Tim Stookesberry
Development editor: Pam Tiberia
Marketing manager: Tracy Landrum
Production supervisor: Richard DeVitto
Print materials consultant: Marilyn Rosenthal
Project manager: Gayle Jaeger, Function Thru Form, Inc.
Design and Electronic Production: Function Thru Form, Inc.
Typeface: Frutiger
Printer and Binder: Quebecor Press Dubuque

Grateful acknowledgment is made for use of the following:

Still Photography: Jeffrey Dunn, Ron Gordon, Judy Mason, Margaret Strom

Additional Photographs: Episode 13 – page 2 left to right, top: © Susanne Buckler, © Scott Cunningham/Liaison International, © Superstock, © Chris Everard/Tony Stone Images; *bottom:* © John Kelly/Tony Stone Images, © Philip Salaverry/Tony Stone Images, © Superstock, © James Jackson/Tony Stone Images; *Episode 14 – page 1 second row, left:* © Chuck Pefley/Tony Stone Images; *third row, center:* © Jeremy Walker/Tony Stone Images; *fourth row, right:* © Paul Avis/Liaison International; *Episode 17 – page 4:* © UPI/Corbis-Bettmann; *Episode 18 – page 1 top left:* © Pete Saloutos/The Stock Market; *top right:* © Jon Feingersh/The Stock Market; *bottom left:* © Tom Stewart/The Stock Market; *bottom right:* © Jon Riley/Tony Stone Images; *page 2 top left:* © Christie's Images/Superstock; *top right:* "Good Neighbors," © Jane Wooster Scott/Superstock; *bottom left:* "Girl at Table," © Michael Mortimer Robinson/ Superstock; *bottom right:* "Performers," © Freshman Brown/Superstock; *Episode 20 – pages 5 and 6:* © UPI/Corbis-Bettmann; *Appendix 2 –* © Mark Andrews/Tony Stone Images; *Appendix 7 – left to right:* © UPI/Corbis-Bettmann, © Superstock, © Jon Feingersh/The Stock Market, © UPI/Corbis-Bettmann

Illustrations: Episode 13 – page 1: Steve Stankiewicz; *Episode 14 – page 6:* Steve Stankiewicz; *Episode 15 – page 1:* Amy Wummer; *Episode 18 – page 6:* Steve Stankiewicz; *Episode 19 – page 1:* Amy Wummer; *page 4:* Andrew Shiff; *Episode 21 – page 3:* Amy Wummer; *Episode 23 – page 2:* Andrew Shiff; *Episode 24 – page 3 and page 6:* Steve Stankiewicz; *Appendix 13–* Steve Stankiewicz

Special thanks to Deborah Gordon, Robin Longshaw, Cheryl Pavlik, and Bill Preston for their contributions to *Conversation Books 1–4.*

Library of Congress Catalog Card No.: 97-75580

International Edition
Copyright © 1998. Exclusive rights by The McGraw-Hill Companies, Inc., for manufacture and export. This book cannot be re-exported from the country to which it is consigned by The McGraw-Hill Companies, Inc. The International Edition is not available in North America.

When ordering this title, use ISBN 0-07-115908-8.

http://www.mhhe.com

Table of Contents

TO THE TEACHER v

A VISUAL TOUR vii

	THEMES	TWO-PAGE ACTIVITY	OPTIONAL PROJECT
EPISODE 13 *JOB HUNTING*	• Giving Directions • International Food • Using Computers	**INFORMATION GAP:** READING BULLETIN BOARDS	Culture Shock *(Appendix 1)*
EPISODE 14 *A BAD DAY*	• Sharing Experiences with a Friend • Having a Bad Day • Making a Date	**GAME:** THE JOB INTERVIEW	Looking for a Job *(Appendix 2)*
EPISODE 15 *A NIGHT OUT*	• Giving Compliments • A First Date • Making Suggestions	**SONG:** GO TO SLEEP	Tourist Attractions *(Appendix 3)*
EPISODE 16 *FIRST DAY OF CLASS*	• Studying with Friends • The First Day of Class • Not Understanding the Teacher	**GAME:** MAKING NEW FRIENDS	Working with Children *(Appendix 4)*
EPISODE 17 *CASEY AT THE BAT*	• Sending and Receiving Flowers • Filling Out Forms • Casey at the Bat, A Famous Poem	**INFORMATION GAP:** SPELLING	Poetry *(Appendix 5)*
EPISODE 18 *THE ART GALLERY*	• Titles of Art Work • Appreciating Art • Money vs. Love	**GAME:** SELLING SOMETHING OF VALUE	Going to an Art Gallery *(Appendix 6)*

	THEMES	TWO-PAGE ACTIVITY	OPTIONAL PROJECT
EPISODE 19 *THE PICNIC*	• Having Fun • Bad Behavior • Going on a Picnic	**INFORMATION GAP:** GETTING CLOSE TO SOMEONE	Team Games *(Appendix 7)*
EPISODE 20 *PREJUDICE*	• Apologizing • Teaching Children Right from Wrong • Appreciating Differences	**INFORMATION GAP:** PREJUDICE IN THE U.S.	Greeting Cards *(Appendix 8)*
EPISODE 21 *A DIFFICULT DECISION*	• A Daily Schedule • Being Stubborn • Missing a Friend	**GAME:** SOLVING PROBLEMS	Making Decisions *(Appendix 9)*
EPISODE 22 *GUITAR LESSONS*	• Marriage • Accepting a Gift • Children and Homework	**INFORMATION GAP:** FAVORS FOR FRIENDS	Television *(Appendix 10)*
EPISODE 23 *THE RETIREMENT PARTY*	• Moving Away • Disciplining Children • Retirement	**GAME:** GOSSIP	International Celebrations *(Appendix 11)*
EPISODE 24 *THE PHONE CALL*	• Parties • Cheer Up! • Bad News	**GAME:** MAKING A TOAST	Dancing *(Appendix 12)*

APPENDICES 1–12   **OPTIONAL PROJECT PAGES, EPISODES 13–24**

APPENDIX 13   **MANIPULATIVES**

To the Teacher

The primary goal of each *Conversation Book* is to help students develop oral communication skills using the themes found in **Connect with English** as a springboard for classroom discussion. This introduction and the following Visual Tour provide important information on how each *Conversation Book* and the corresponding video episodes can be successfully combined to teach English as a second or foreign language.

LANGUAGE SKILLS:

Each *Conversation Book* has 12 chapters which contain a variety of pair, group, team, and whole-class activities that are based on important issues and ideas from the corresponding video episodes.

The activity types vary with each chapter but generally include an assortment of role-plays, discussions, opinion surveys, games, interviews, and question- naires. In each chapter, a special two-page section is devoted to longer games, information gaps, and songs from the **Connect with English** sound- track. Students also have the opportunity to work on special project pages found in appendices in the back of the book. These projects provide students with the opportunity to explore key themes outside of the classroom.

THEMATIC ORGANIZATION:

Events and issues that are familiar and important to all ESL/EFL learners have been purposely included in the **Connect with English** story. These topics were carefully chosen for their relevant cultural content, and they provide a rich context for the communicative activities found in the *Conversation Books.* As students watch the video story and become familiar with the events and characters, the *Conversation Books* provide a framework within which students can freely discuss the ideas presented in each episode. Throughout *Conversation Books 1-4,* students are given the opportunity to explore such varied themes as the following:

- Pursuing Your Dream
- Making Future Plans
- Looking for a Job
- Making New Friends
- Money vs. Love
- Having Fun
- Apologizing
- Making a Difficult Decision
- Gossip
- Divorce and Remarriage
- Regrets
- Anger
- Making Compromises
- Spending Money
- Adulthood
- Best Friends
- Managing Priorities
- Parenting
- Helping Others
- The Death of a Loved One
- Dedication
- Moving
- Holidays
- Life Lessons

PROFICIENCY LEVEL:

The activities found in each *Conversation Book* are designed for use with high-beginning to intermediate students. Special icons are used to identify the difficulty level of each activity in the book. These icons help teachers tailor the activities for the needs of students at different levels of language proficiency.

 Arrows pointing up indicate that the difficulty of an activity can be increased.

 Arrows pointing down indicate that an activity can be simplified.

 Arrows pointing in both directions indicate that the difficulty level of the activity can be either increased or simplified.

Detailed teaching suggestions on modifying each activity are found in the accompanying Instructor's Manual.

OPTIONS FOR USE:

The *Conversation Books* are specifically designed for classroom use. While it is assumed that students have watched the corresponding video episode at least once before attempting the activities in the book, it is not necessary to have classroom access to a TV or VCR. Teachers may choose to show the video during class time, or they can assign students to watch the video episodes prior to class, either in a library, language lab, or at home. Class time can then be used for completion of the activities found in the *Conversation Book*.

Each *Conversation Book* can be used as the sole text in any course that emphasizes oral communication skills. Teachers also have the option of combining the *Conversation Books* with other corresponding texts in the **Connect with English** print package:

- *Video Comprehension Books 1-4* contain a variety of comprehension activities that enhance and solidify students' understanding of main events in the video story.

- *Grammar Guides 1-4* provide multilevel practice in grammar structures and vocabulary items derived from the **Connect with English** video episodes.

- *Connections Readers* (16 titles) offer students graded reading practice based on the **Connect with English** story.

- *Video Scripts 1-4* include the exact dialogue from each of the video episodes and can be used in a variety of ways in conjunction with any of the other texts in the **Connect with English** program.

For additional information on these and other materials in the **Connect with English** program, please refer to the inside back cover of this book.

A VISUAL TOUR OF THIS TEXT

This visual tour is designed to introduce the key features of *Conversation Book 2*. The primary focus of each *Conversation Book* is to help students develop oral communication skills within the context of the *Connect with English* story. *Conversation Book 2* corresponds to episodes 13–24 of *Connect with English*, and it presents an assortment of activities dealing with various aspects of communication, including explaining, questioning, interviewing, reporting, paraphrasing, describing, stating feelings/opinions, and more.

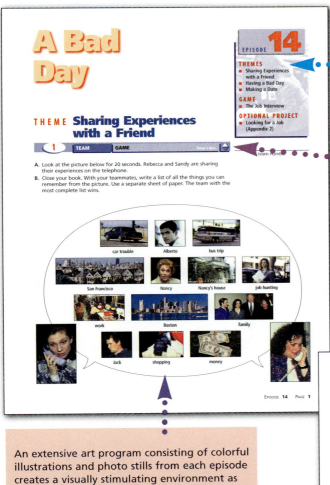

Themes drawn directly from the video episodes are listed at the start of each chapter. In Episode 14, activities are based on the themes of Sharing Experiences with a Friend, Having a Bad Day, and Making a Date. A two-page game is devoted to the topic of job interviews, and an optional project encourages students to research different methods of finding a job.

Multilevel Activities

Special icons are used to show the difficulty level of each activity in the book. These icons are designed to help teachers tailor the activities to the needs of a multilevel group of students. An arrow pointing up ▲ indicates that the difficulty of an activity can be increased, while an arrow pointing down ▼ indicates that an activity can be simplified for lower-level students. Arrows pointing in both directions ◆ indicate that the activity can be adjusted in either direction. Detailed teaching suggestions for how to change the level of each activity in *Conversation Book 2* are included in the accompanying Instructor's Manual.

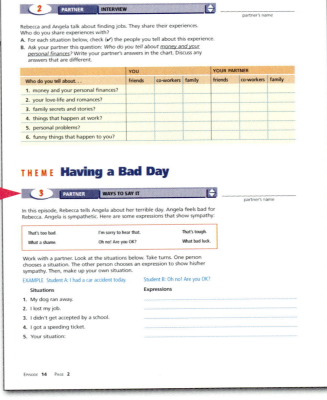

An extensive art program consisting of colorful illustrations and photo stills from each episode creates a visually stimulating environment as the basis for many communicative activities.

A regular feature of the *Conversation Books*, **Ways to Say It** activities introduce students to several common expressions used in daily conversation. Special effort has been made to include high-frequency, natural language which reflects the language used in the video episodes and in everyday speech in the United States and Canada.

A VISUAL TOUR   vii

Activity bars identify the start of each numbered activity and indicate whether the activity is designed for pairs, groups, teams, or whole-class participation. Descriptors such as **Discussion, Interview,** or **Role-Play** alert teachers to the type of activity that follows.

Spaces that allow students to indicate partner name, group number, and team number make it easier for students and teachers to keep track of student collaborations. Group and team numbers are also useful when different groups are asked to compare and contrast survey or discussion results with one another.

What About You? activities provide open-ended questions that encourage students to express their personal feelings and opinions as they relate to the themes presented in the story. These activities create a springboard for more sophisticated discussions among students who are at higher levels of oral proficiency. **What About You?** activities can also be used as optional writing assignments.

Variety of Activity Types
Each chapter contains a variety of activity types that feature different student combinations and communicative objectives. For example, Activity 4 features an interview about bad days, Activity 5 asks partners to perform a role-play, and Activity 6 features a group discussion on opinions related to making dates.

---

4 — PARTNER — INTERVIEW

partner's name

When you have a bad day, what helps you feel better?
A. Check (✔) the things that help you feel better. Under *Details*, write more specific information about what you do to feel better.
B. Ask your partner this question: Does *relaxing help you feel better?* Check (✔) your partner's answers. Find out the details and write them down.

EXAMPLE

Does ____ help you feel better?	Yes	No	Details
relaxing	✔		I listen to soft music.

Does ____ help feel better?	YOU			YOUR PARTNER		
	Yes	No	Details	Yes	No	Details
relaxing						
eating						
exercising						
talking						
being alone						

C. Ask your partner this question: *What else helps you feel better?*
Write your partner's answer here. _____

What About YOU?
1. Can you remember a bad day in your life? What happened?
2. Did anything help you feel better?
3. Did you ever help someone else who had a bad day? What did you do?

THEME **Making a Date**

5 — PARTNER — ROLE-PLAY

partner's name

Work with a partner. Practice making a date with a friend. Call your partner on the phone. Act out the conversation. Use the phrases below for help. Then, switch roles.

Ways to ask for a date:	Are you free *tomorrow night/Saturday. . .*? Would you like to *have lunch with me/ see a movie/come to a party. . .*?
Ways to accept a date:	That sounds like fun. Yes, I'd like that.
Ways to reject a date:	I'm sorry, but I can't. I'm afraid I already have plans.
Ways to end the conversation:	Great! Can I *pick you up/meet you somewhere. . .*? OK, then. Maybe another time. Good-bye.

6 — GROUP — DISCUSSION

group number

A. How do you feel about making a date? Read the sentences below and check (✔) *I agree* or *I disagree.*

	I agree	I disagree
1. It's OK for a woman to ask a man for a date.		
2. A person should call at least a week in advance to make a date.		
3. The person who makes the date should have a plan for the date.		
4. The person who makes the date should pay for everything.		
5. If a person says "no" to your invitation, you shouldn't ask him or her for a date again.		
6. It's OK to ask a person on a date, even if he or she already has a boyfriend or girlfriend.		
7. It's OK to make a date with someone who is older than you.		

B. Discuss the answers to these questions with your group.
■ Which statements does everyone agree with? _____
■ Are there any statements that everyone disagrees with? _____
■ Are you surprised by any of your group members' answers? _____
If so, ask these questions:
Why do you think that? or *Could you explain that?*

EPISODE **14** PAGE **4**

A VISUAL TOUR **viii**

Two-Page Activity

Each episode contains an extended theme which is covered in a longer, two-page activity. These themes are developed into games, information gaps, or activities based on songs from the *Connect with English* soundtrack.

This two-page game, "The Job Interview," is based on Rebecca's job interview experiences in San Francisco. In this game, students are involved in the creation of the game cards. This participation simultaneously increases motivation and reviews important concepts and vocabulary related to the story.

Step-by-step explanations and clear, concise examples provide necessary structure and format as students prepare and create game cards. Game instructions are presented in an organized fashion that takes students through each step of play.

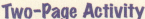

GAME: The Job Interview

7 GROUP — GAME

You're going for a job interview. If you do and say the right things—and you have good luck—you'll get the job!

Get Ready to Play

Step One
Divide into groups of two to four players. Each group of players will need a coin.

Step Two
Each player will need a piece of paper. Cut (or fold and tear) the paper into six or more pieces. These will be the game cards. Game cards look like this:

- You answer the interviewer's questions well. GO AHEAD 2
- You speak with confidence. GO AHEAD 1
- You have ketchup on your shirt. GO BACK 1
- You forgot to bring your résumé. GO BACK 2

Each player will need to make three GO AHEAD cards and three GO BACK cards. Make them for one or two spaces. You can work alone or with others to think of ideas for the game cards. Here are some examples:

Topics for cards	GO AHEAD...	GO BACK...
a. How you look	You are well dressed.	Your hair is very messy.
b. How you speak	You speak clearly.	You speak too softly.
c. How you act	You seem serious about the job.	You are chewing bubble gum.
d. Your application or résumé	Your résumé is very neat.	Your application is incomplete.
e. Your experience or references	You have excellent references.	You have no work experience.

Step Three
Shuffle the game cards, and put them in a pile face down on the table. Turn to the game board on page 6. Cut out the markers on Appendix 13. Put the markers on START.

Play the Game
- Decide who will go first. That player tosses the coin. If the coin lands heads up, that player moves ahead one space. If the coin lands tails up, that player moves ahead two spaces.
- If there is something written on the space where you land, read it aloud. Follow the directions. You might have to move ahead, move back, or draw a card.
- If you draw a card, read it aloud. Follow the directions on the card. You can draw only one card on each turn.
- If the card tells you to go AHEAD or BACK to a space, move your marker and stay there. Don't follow the directions on that space. Wait for your next turn.
- If you land on a FREE space, stay there and wait for your next turn.
- The next player tosses the coin, and play continues.
- The first person to reach YOU'RE HIRED! gets the job and wins the game.

EPISODE 14 PAGE 5

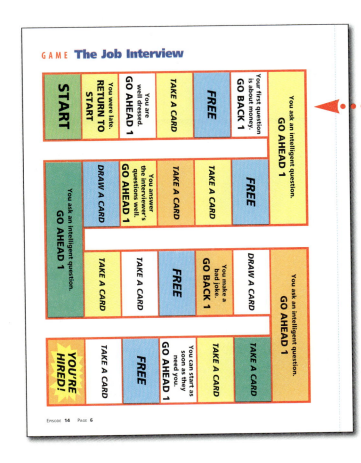

Each book contains colorful game boards that are removable, making them easy for students to use on a desk or tabletop. Game pieces and markers for students to cut out and use are found in Appendix 13 at the back of the book.

Cut out die. Fold here and tape together.

A VISUAL TOUR ix

Project Page

Optional project pages correspond to each episode and are found in appendices located at the back of the book. Project pages contain research-oriented activities or community surveys and polls based on important themes from each episode. These projects reinforce the communicative nature of the *Conversation Books* and invite students to expand their learning and conversation to areas beyond the classroom environment.

On this project page, students use newspapers to find out what kinds of jobs are listed in the employment section. Project pages throughout the *Conversation Books* encourage students to use a variety of research tools, including books, encyclopedias, newspapers, magazines, almanacs, and the Internet.

In this community survey, students interview people from outside the class in order to determine different methods of finding a job. As students gather information, they are often asked to synthesize their findings with those of their classmates in order to gain a complete understanding of the theme.

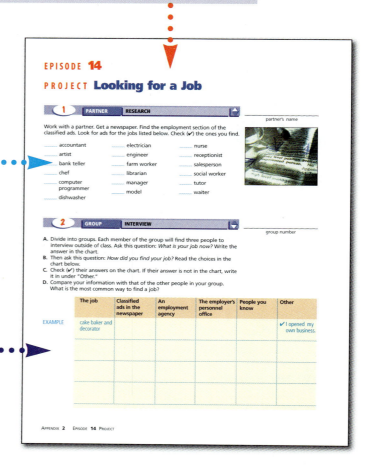

A VISUAL TOUR   x

Job Hunting

EPISODE 13

THEMES
- Giving Directions
- International Food
- Using Computers

INFORMATION GAP
- Reading Bulletin Boards

OPTIONAL PROJECT
- Culture Shock (Appendix 1)

THEME Giving Directions

1 PARTNER   WAYS TO SAY IT

partner's name

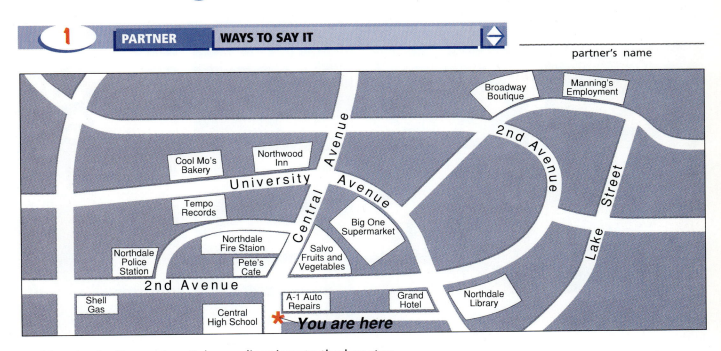

In this episode, Nancy gives Rebecca directions to the bus stop. She says, *"Take a right. Go two blocks. You'll see the bus stop."*

Here are some other useful phrases for giving directions:

Turn (take a) right/left at the corner.	**Keep going until** you see the bakery.	**It's near** the school.
Go straight for three **blocks**.	**It's across from** the library.	**It's on the corner.**
Go down 2nd Ave. **until** the lights.	**It will be on your** right/left.	

With a partner, take turns asking for and giving directions to the buildings on the map above. Use the phrases in the box.

EXAMPLE
Student A: How do I get to Tempo Records?
Student B: Go straight on Central Avenue for three blocks. Turn left at University Avenue. Keep going straight. Tempo Records will be on your left. It's across from Cool Mo's Bakery.

EPISODE 13   PAGE 1

2 GROUP GAME

group number

Divide into groups. One person gives directions to a building on the map on page 1. The first person to find the building wins. The winner gives directions to the next place.

What About You?
1. Do you get lost easily?
2. Where did you get lost recently?
3. Do you prefer to ask directions or read a map?

THEME International Food

3 PARTNER INTERVIEW

partner's name

Chinese _____   French _____   American _____   Japanese _____

Mexican _____   Italian _____   German _____   Indian _____

In this episode, Melaku makes a special Ethiopian meal for Rebecca and the others.

A. Look at the pictures above. Do you eat any of these international foods? Put a check (✔) next to the ones you've tried.

B. Answer these questions. Then ask a partner. Write your partner's answers.

	You	Your partner
1. Which kind of food is your favorite?		
2. Which kind of food is your least favorite?		
3. Which food do you eat the most often?		
4. Which food do you never eat?		
5. Do you have a favorite kind of food that is not on this page? What is it?		

EPISODE 13   PAGE 2

PARTNER   SHARE

_____
partner's name

A. Write about your favorite meal. It can be from your country, or it can be any kind of international food that you like. Then, tell your partner about this meal.

EXAMPLE My favorite meal is _macaroni and cheese_.
It's made with _cheese, pasta, milk, and butter_.
It's served _hot_.
I eat it for _dinner_.
I like to eat _green beans or beets_ with it.

Your favorite meal

My favorite meal is _____.	I eat it for _____.
It's made with _____.	I like to eat _____ with it.
It's served <u>hot/cold</u>.	

B. Listen to your partner describe his or her favorite meal. Write what your partner says in the lines below.

Your partner's favorite meal

His/her favorite meal is _____.	He/she eats it for _____.
It's made with _____.	He/she likes to eat _____ with it.
It's served <u>hot/cold</u>.	

1. What do you normally eat for breakfast?
2. Which foods do you like to cook?
3. Which common foods do you dislike?

THEME Using Computers

 PARTNER   CATEGORIES

_____
partner's name

In this episode, Rebecca needs computer skills in order to get the job she wants.

A. How often do these people use computers at work? Write each job in one of the three categories below. Compare your answers with those of a partner.

B. Pick three jobs. Tell your partner what a computer is used for in each job.

factory worker	teacher	secretary	architect	airplane pilot
telephone operator	doctor	lawyer	bus driver	engineer
car mechanic	librarian	carpenter	writer	photographer

Sometimes   **Often**   **Very often**

EPISODE **13**   PAGE **3**

6 GROUP DISCUSSION

group number

How do you feel about using computers?

A. If you use a computer, answer the questions in *Survey A*. If you don't use a computer, answer the questions in *Survey B*. Check (✔) your answers.

B. Form a group with other people who have answered the same survey questions. Answer the discussion questions together. Share your results with the class.

Survey A

	Yes	No
1. I use a computer at work.		
2. I use a computer at home.		
3. I think computers are fun.		
4. I use computers to play games.		
5. I keep important information on my computer.		
6. I know a lot about computers.		
7. I use a computer for the Internet.		

Discussion questions—Survey A

1. Where do more people use computers—at home or at work? _____
2. How many people use a computer to play games? _____
3. How many people use the Internet? _____
4. Who uses a computer the most in your group? _____

Survey B

	Yes	No
1. I'm interested in computers.		
2. I need a computer.		
3. I don't need a computer.		
4. I don't like computers.		
5. I'm afraid of computers.		
6. I *have* to learn how to use a computer.		
7. I *want* to learn how to use a computer.		

Discussion questions—Survey B

1. Who is interested in computers? _____
2. How many people need a computer? _____
3. How many people want to learn how to use a computer? _____
4. Are more people *interested in* computers or *afraid of* computers? _____

EPISODE 13 PAGE 4

INFORMATION GAP Reading Bulletin Boards

7 PARTNER — INFORMATION GAP

STUDENT A

partner's name

Work with a partner. One of you works on this page. The other works on page 6. Don't look at your partner's page.

In this episode, Rebecca looks on a bulletin board for job openings. Each of the bulletin board messages below is missing some important information.
Your partner has the information you need in order to complete each message.
Ask your partner these questions:
- What's the position?
- What are the hours?
- Who do I contact?
- What are the requirements?

Write the missing information in the spaces below.

HELP WANTED
Position: _____
Hours: EVENINGS
Contact: CALL 555-1151 — ASK FOR JOHN.
Requirements: _____

HELP WANTED
Position: Cook at College Dining Hall
Hours: Full-time
Contact: Sherry, Manager
Requirements: _____

HELP WANTED
Position: Tour Guide
Hours: _____
Contact: Bay City Tours
Requirements: Must know city of San Francisco, tourist attractions.

HELP WANTED
Position: Female Singer
Hours: Weekend evenings
Contact: _____
Requirements: Must play guitar and sing pop music.

HELP WANTED
Position: Receptionist
Hours: _____
Contact: Mr. Gleason at Bender Associates
Requirements: Must have good typing and computer skills.

HELP WANTED
Position: _____
Hours: Mornings only, Wed–Sat
Contact: Susan at 555-8759
Requirements: Must have a car.

HELP WANTED
Position: Waiter/Waitress at Derby's 24 Hour Restaurant
Hours: 8 a.m.–4 p.m. Saturdays and Sundays
Contact: Manager at Derby's, 623 Lake Street
Requirements: _____

HELP WANTED
Position: _____
Hours: 12 HOURS PER WEEK
Contact: Marvin, Room 602, S.F. College of Music
Requirements: MUST HAVE PREVIOUS TEACHING EXPERIENCE.

8 PARTNER — DISCUSSION

With your partner, choose the best jobs for Rebecca. Circle them. Discuss your answers with the rest of the class.

EPISODE 13   PAGE 5

INFORMATION GAP Reading Bulletin Boards

7 PARTNER — INFORMATION GAP

STUDENT B — Work with a partner. One of you works on this page. The other works on page 5. Don't look at your partner's page.

_____
partner's name

In this episode, Rebecca looks on a bulletin board for job openings. Each of the bulletin board messages below is missing some important information.
Your partner has the information you need in order to complete each message.
Ask your partner these questions:
- What's the position?
- What are the hours?
- Who do I contact?
- What are the requirements?

Write the missing information in the spaces below.

8 PARTNER — DISCUSSION

With your partner, choose the best jobs for Rebecca. Circle them. Discuss your answers with the rest of the class.

EPISODE **13** PAGE **6**

EPISODE 14

THEMES
- Sharing Experiences with a Friend
- Having a Bad Day
- Making a Date

GAME
- The Job Interview

OPTIONAL PROJECT
- Looking for a Job (Appendix 2)

THEME: Sharing Experiences with a Friend

| 1 | TEAM | GAME | Time: 5 min. |

team number

A. Look at the picture below for 20 seconds. Rebecca and Sandy are sharing their experiences on the telephone.

B. Close your book. With your teammates, write a list of all the things you can remember from the picture. Use a separate sheet of paper. The team with the most complete list wins.

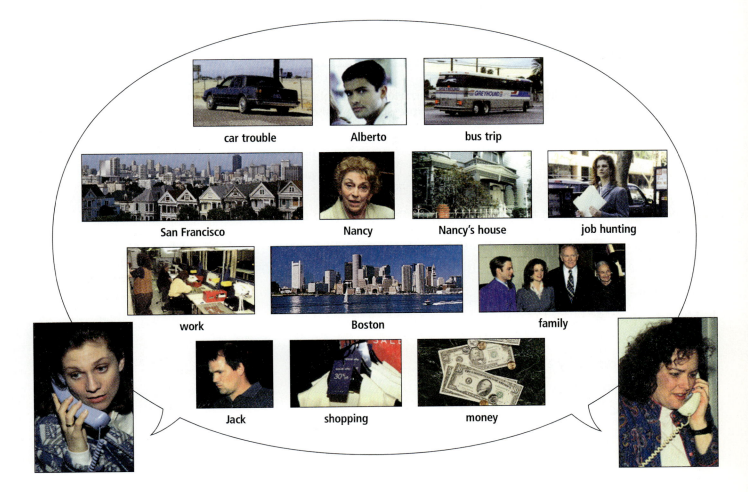

EPISODE 14 PAGE 1

2 PARTNER INTERVIEW

partner's name

Rebecca and Angela talk about finding jobs. They share their experiences.
Who do you share experiences with?

A. For each situation below, check (✔) the people you tell about this experience.

B. Ask your partner this question: *Who do you tell about <u>money and your personal finances</u>?* Write your partner's answers in the chart. Discuss any answers that are different.

Who do you tell about. . .	YOU			YOUR PARTNER		
	friends	co-workers	family	friends	co-workers	family
1. money and your personal finances?						
2. your love-life and romances?						
3. family secrets and stories?						
4. things that happen at work?						
5. personal problems?						
6. funny things that happen to you?						

THEME Having a Bad Day

3 PARTNER WAYS TO SAY IT

partner's name

In this episode, Rebecca tells Angela about her terrible day. Angela feels bad for Rebecca. Angela is sympathetic. Here are some expressions that show sympathy:

That's too bad.	I'm sorry to hear that.	That's tough.
What a shame.	Oh no! Are you OK?	What bad luck.

Work with a partner. Look at the situations below. Take turns. One person chooses a situation. The other person chooses an expression to show his/her sympathy. Then, make up your own situation.

EXAMPLE Student A: I had a car accident today.   Student B: Oh no! Are you OK?

Situations

Expressions

1. My dog ran away.

2. I lost my job.

3. I didn't get accepted by a school.

4. I got a speeding ticket.

5. Your situation:

EPISODE **14**   PAGE **2**

4 PARTNER INTERVIEW

_____
partner's name

When you have a bad day, what helps you feel better?

A. Check (✔) the things that help you feel better. Under *Details*, write more specific information about what you do to feel better.

B. Ask your partner this question: Does <u>relaxing</u> *help you feel better*? Check (✔) your partner's answers. Find out the details and write them down.

EXAMPLE

Does _____ help you feel better?	Yes	No	Details
relaxing	✔		I listen to soft music.

Does _____ help feel better?	YOU			YOUR PARTNER		
	Yes	No	Details	Yes	No	Details
relaxing						
eating						
exercising						
talking						
being alone						

C. Ask your partner this question: *What else helps you feel better?*

Write your partner's answer here. _____

_____

_____

1. Can you remember a bad day in your life? What happened?
2. Did anything help you feel better?
3. Did you ever help someone else who had a bad day? What did you do?

EPISODE **14** PAGE **3**

THEME Making a Date

5	**PARTNER**	**ROLE-PLAY**	

partner's name

Work with a partner. Practice making a date with a friend. Call your partner
on the phone. Act out the conversation. Use the phrases below for help.
Then, switch roles.

Ways to ask for a date: Are you free *tomorrow night/Saturday*. . .?
Would you like to *have lunch with me/*
see a movie/come to a party. . .?

Ways to accept a date: That sounds like fun.
Yes, I'd like that.

Ways to reject a date: I'm sorry, but I can't.
I'm afraid I already have plans.

Ways to end the conversation: Great! Can I *pick you up/meet you somewhere*. . .?
OK, then. Maybe another time. Good-bye.

6	**GROUP**	**DISCUSSION**	

group number

A. How do you feel about making a date? Read the sentences below and
check (✔) *I agree* or *I disagree*.

	I agree	I disagree
1. It's OK for a woman to ask a man for a date.	_____	_____
2. A person should call at least a week in advance to make a date.	_____	_____
3. The person who makes the date should have a plan for the date.	_____	_____
4. The person who makes the date should pay for everything.	_____	_____
5. If a person says "no" to your invitation, you shouldn't ask him or her for a date again.	_____	_____
6. It's OK to ask a person on a date, even if he or she already has a boyfriend or girlfriend.	_____	_____
7. It's OK to make a date with someone who is older than you.	_____	_____

B. Discuss the answers to these questions with your group.

■ Which statements does everyone agree with? _____

■ Are there any statements that everyone

disagrees with? _____

■ Are you surprised by any of your group members' answers? _____

If so, ask these questions:
Why do you think that? or *Could you explain that?*

EPISODE **14**   PAGE **4**

GAME The Job Interview

7 GROUP   GAME

You're going for a job interview. If you do and say the right things—and you have good luck—you'll get the job!

Get Ready to Play

Step One
Divide into groups of two to four players. Each group of players will need a coin.

Step Two
Each player will need a piece of paper. Cut (or fold and tear) the paper into six or more pieces. These will be the game cards. Game cards look like this:

   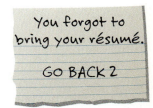

Each player will need to make three GO AHEAD cards and three GO BACK cards. Make them for one or two spaces. You can work alone or with others to think of ideas for the game cards. Here are some examples:

Topics for cards	GO AHEAD...	GO BACK...
a. How you look	You are well dressed.	Your hair is very messy.
b. How you speak	You speak clearly.	You speak too softly.
c. How you act	You seem serious about the job.	You are chewing bubble gum.
d. Your application or résumé	Your résumé is very neat.	Your application is incomplete.
e. Your experience or references	You have excellent references.	You have no work experience.

Step Three
Shuffle the game cards, and put them in a pile face down on the table. Turn to the game board on page 6. Cut out the markers on Appendix 13. Put the markers on START.

Play the Game
- Decide who will go first. That player tosses the coin. If the coin lands heads up, that player moves ahead one space. If the coin lands tails up, that player moves ahead two spaces.
- If there is something written on the space where you land, read it aloud. Follow the directions. You might have to move ahead, move back, or draw a card.
- If you draw a card, read it aloud. Follow the directions on the card. You can draw only one card on each turn.
- If the card tells you to go AHEAD or BACK to a space, move your marker and stay there. Don't follow the directions on that space. Wait for your next turn.
- If you land on a FREE space, stay there and wait for your next turn.
- The next player tosses the coin, and play continues.
- The first person to reach YOU'RE HIRED! gets the job and wins the game.

EPISODE **14**   PAGE **5**

GAME The Job Interview

START

RETURN TO START
You were late.

GO AHEAD 1
You are well dressed.

TAKE A CARD

FREE

GO BACK 1
Your first question is about money.

GO AHEAD 1
You ask an intelligent question.

DRAW A CARD

GO AHEAD 1
You answer the interviewer's questions well.

TAKE A CARD

TAKE A CARD

FREE

GO AHEAD 1
You ask an intelligent question.

TAKE A CARD

TAKE A CARD

FREE

GO BACK 1
You make a bad joke.

DRAW A CARD

GO AHEAD 1
You ask an intelligent question.

YOU'RE HIRED!

TAKE A CARD

FREE

GO AHEAD 1
You can start as soon as they need you.

TAKE A CARD

TAKE A CARD

EPISODE **14** PAGE **6**

A Night Out

EPISODE 15

THEMES
- Giving Compliments
- A First Date
- Making Suggestions

SONG
- Go to Sleep

OPTIONAL PROJECT
- Tourist Attractions (Appendix 3)

THEME Giving Compliments

1 GROUP ROLE-PLAY

_____
group number

In this episode, Alberto sees Rebecca in San Francisco. He gives her a compliment. He tells her, "You look terrific!" Read the compliments that this class gives the teacher.

A. Divide into groups. One person from each group plays the teacher. The rest of the group plays the students.
B. Each student gives the teacher a compliment. Write your group's compliments on a separate sheet of paper so you won't repeat any.
C. The teacher will decide which compliment he/she likes best. The person who gave that compliment will play the teacher next.

2 GROUP DISCUSSION

_____
group number

A. Divide into groups. Discuss the following questions with the people in your group.
- When is it appropriate to give someone (a teacher, a friend, a co-worker, and so on) a compliment?
- When isn't it appropriate to give someone a compliment?

B. Talk as a class. Your teacher will write each groups' answers to these questions on the board.

EPISODE **15** PAGE **1**

3 PARTNER   INTERVIEW

partner's name

Answer these questions about compliments. Then ask your partner about his/her answers. Write down your partner's answers in the chart below.

You		Your partner	
Do you like getting compliments?		Do you like getting compliments?	
What's the best compliment you have ever gotten?		What's the best compliment you have ever gotten?	
Who compliments you the most (friend, parent, co-worker, and so on)?		Who compliments you the most (friend, parent, co-worker, and so on)?	
Who do you compliment the most?		Who do you compliment the most?	
What's a compliment that you could give someone in the class?		What's a compliment that you could give someone in the class?	

THEME A First Date

 4 GROUP   DISCUSSION

group number

In the United States, eating at a restaurant ("going out to eat") is a popular thing to do on a first date.

A. With your group, think of three other things to do on a first date. Write your answers below.

Things to do on a first date

1. _____
2. _____
3. _____

B. Find out what the most popular "first date" activity is in your group. Write it below.

_____

C. Compare your answers with those of another group. Did you have different answers?

EPISODE 15   PAGE 2

5 GROUP DEBATE

group number

In this episode, Rebecca and Alberto go on a date. Alberto takes Rebecca to a restaurant, but he doesn't tell her that she'll meet his parents.

A. Divide into two groups. If you agree with Opinion 1 below, join group 1. If you agree with Opinion 2, join group 2.
B. With your group, make a list of reasons to support your opinion. Be ready to explain each one.
C. Take turns. Each group has five minutes to present its ideas.

Opinion 1: It's OK that Alberto takes Rebecca to meet his parents on the first date. Rebecca shouldn't worry about it.

Reasons

1. _____
2. _____
3. _____
4. _____
5. _____
6. _____

Opinion 2: It's not OK that Alberto takes Rebecca to meet his parents on the first date. It's not fair to surprise her.

Reasons

1. _____
2. _____
3. _____
4. _____
5. _____
6. _____

1. What's your idea of a perfect first date?
2. Have you ever gone on a "blind" date? (A blind date is a date with someone you've never seen or met before.)
3. Would you go on a blind date?
4. At what age should a person begin to date?

EPISODE 15   PAGE 3

T H E M E Making Suggestions

---

6 **PARTNER** **WAYS TO SAY IT**

_____
partner's name

In this episode, Alberto, Ramón, and Mr. Mendoza all give suggestions to Rebecca. Here are some ways that people make suggestions in English:

You should study harder.	**How about** going to the movies?
Why don't you quit your job?	**You could** talk to the teacher if you're having trouble.
I recommend the hamburgers here.	**You might want** to see a doctor.

Work with a partner. Look at the situations below. Take turns. One person chooses a situation. The other person uses one of the expressions above to make a suggestion. Then, make up your own situation.

EXAMPLE   Student A: My math class is very difficult.   Student B: You might want to get a tutor.

Situations   **Expressions**

1. I'm hungry.   _____

2. I have a cold.   _____

3. I'm bored.   _____

4. I want to lose weight.   _____

5. I want to meet new friends.   _____

6. Your situation: _____

---

7 **GROUP** **SHARE**

_____
group number

A. What's a suggestion that you've gotten? In the box below, write the suggestion and who gave it to you. Look at the example.

EXAMPLE   My mother gave me a suggestion. She said, "You should save a little money every week." It was a good suggestion because I saved a lot of money.

_____ gave me a suggestion.
He/she said "_____

_____

_____."
It was a good/bad suggestion because _____

_____.

B. Read your suggestion to your group.

Did anyone in your group get a suggestion that is similar to yours?

What was it? _____

EPISODE **15**   PAGE **4**

SONG Go to Sleep

 PARTNER | **SONG**

_____
partner's name

A. Rebecca sings a song for Alberto called "Go to Sleep." Rebecca's mother taught her the song. With your partner, look at the words to the song and discuss them. Answer the questions below.

Go to sleep. The stars are brightly shining.

Go to sleep. The moon is on the rise.

Our life's a dream. We barely know we're dreaming.

Till I see the light that's shining in your eyes.

Till I see the light that's shining in your eyes.

1. In the song, what time of day is it?

2. In the song, who do you think the singer is singing to? Explain.

3. Is this a happy song or a sad song? Explain.

4. Rebecca's mother called this song "Go to Sleep." Can you think of other possible titles for the song?

EPISODE **15**   PAGE **5**

9	**PARTNER**	**SONG**	

partner's name

A. Have you learned any songs, stories, or phrases from your parents or grandparents?

Write your favorite one below.

Song, story, or phrase from your family

_____
_____
_____
_____
_____
_____
_____
_____
_____
_____
_____

B. Your partner will read what he/she has written. Complete the activities below. Then, switch places. Read what you have written to your partner. He/she will do the activities below.

1. Listen to what your partner reads to you. What family tradition did your partner write about? Check (✔) the answer.

   _____ a family song

   _____ a family story

   _____ a family phrase

   _____ other _____
   _____
   _____
   _____

2. Write three sentences about what your partner tells you. For example, these three sentences are about what Rebecca tells Alberto.

   1. Rebecca has a family song.
   2. Her mother wrote the song.
   3. Rebecca sang the song to her little brother Kevin.

   Write your sentences here. Then read them to your partner. Your partner will tell you if you have understood everything correctly.

   1. _____
   2. _____
   3. _____

1. Did anyone sing to you when you were a child?
2. What family traditions does your family have?
3. What traditions will you give to your children?

EPISODE 15   PAGE 6

First Day of Class

EPISODE 16

THEMES
- Studying with Friends
- The First Day of Class
- Not Understanding the Teacher

GAME
- Making New Friends

OPTIONAL PROJECT
- Working with Children (Appendix 4)

THEME Studying with Friends

1 CLASS GAME Time: 10 min.

What are the study habits of your classmates? Ask these questions to find out.

A. Read the list of survey questions below. Ask your teacher to explain any of the questions that you don't understand.

B. When your teacher tells you, stand up and walk around the classroom. Ask your classmates the questions in the survey. If someone answers *yes* to a question, write his or her name in the space.

C. Keep asking questions until you have names in all the spaces or until your teacher says there is no more time. The person with the most names wins.

Question	Name
1. Do you listen to music while you study?	
2. Do you eat while you study?	
3. Do you study every night?	
4. Do you take notes while you study?	
5. Do you study late at night?	
6. Do you study right before class?	
7. Do you like to study?	
8. Do you prefer to study alone?	
9. Do you study at the same time every day?	
10. Do you study with a friend?	
11. Do you study at home?	
12. Do you study in the library?	

2 PARTNER DISCUSSION

_____
partner's name

In this episode, Rebecca and Bill decide to study together. When you're going to study with a friend, it's important to have similar opinions on study habits.

A. Discuss the study habits in the list below with your partner.

B. Write a *G* next to the *good* habits and *B* next to the *bad* habits. If you can't agree on an answer, write a *U* in the space. This means that you are undecided.

C. When you're finished, join another pair. Compare answers. Do you all agree on the same good and bad habits? What habits did the other pair label with a *U*?

_____ studying at the library   _____ underlining important information in your book

_____ taking notes while you read   _____ studying late at night

_____ studying the night before an exam _____ studying every night

_____ studying with a classmate   _____ studying with the radio or television on

_____ eating while you study   _____ studying a week before an exam

THEME The First Day of Class

3 CLASS BRAINSTORM

In this episode, Rebecca goes to her first day of class at the San Francisco School of Music. What do people usually do on the first day of class?

A. With your classmates, make a list of all of the things that a person does on the first day of class. Use this list of words for ideas.

schedule	talk	teacher	classroom
classmates	time	homework	paper
book	ask	tell	

B. Write your classmates' ideas in the space below. Ask the teacher or another student in the class to make a "master list" on the board.

_____   _____
_____   _____
_____   _____
_____   _____
_____   _____
_____   _____
_____   _____

4 PARTNER INTERVIEW

_____
partner's name

Think about a class that you had in the past. What do you remember about the first day? Be ready to tell your partner about it.

Step One
Ask each other the questions below. Write what your partner says.

1. Where was the class?
2. What was the teacher's name?
3. What kind of class was it?
4. Did you know any other students in the class?
5. How did you feel on the first day?
6. Your own question:

Step Two
In the space provided, write a short paragraph about the first day of class that your partner described.

Step Three
When you're done, read what you have written to your partner. Your partner will tell you if you have understood everything correctly.

1. How do you feel on the first day of class? Are you nervous or excited?
2. What do you remember about the first day of this class?
3. What's the most important thing to learn on the first day of class?

EPISODE 16   PAGE 3

THEME Not Understanding the Teacher

5 PARTNER — WAYS TO SAY IT

_____
partner's name

In this episode, Rebecca and Bill think their class is very difficult. Here are some expressions to use when you don't understand something:

> I'm sorry, I didn't understand that.   What did you say?   I don't get it.
>
> Could you repeat that, please?   I beg your pardon?

Work with a partner. Look at the situations below. Take turns. One person chooses a situation. The other person chooses an expression to show that he/she doesn't understand. Then, make up your own situation.

Situations **Expressions**

EXAMPLE You didn't hear the date of the exam. Could you repeat that, please?

1. You don't understand the assignment. _____
2. Your teacher is speaking too fast. _____
3. Your classmate asks you a question but you didn't hear him/her. _____
4. Your friend tells a story you don't understand. _____
5. Your situation: _____

6 PARTNER — INTERVIEW

_____
partner's name

What do you do when you don't understand the teacher?

A. Check (✔) your answers on the list below.

B. Ask your partner the things he/she does. Check (✔) your partner's answers.

C. Discuss any answers that are different. Ask the question: Why <u>do/don't</u> you do that?

What do you do when you don't understand the teacher?	You		Your partner	
	Yes	No	Yes	No
1. Do you get mad at yourself?	❏	❏	❏	❏
2. Do you get angry at the teacher?	❏	❏	❏	❏
3. Do you raise your hand to ask a question?	❏	❏	❏	❏
4. Do you talk to the teacher after class?	❏	❏	❏	❏
5. Do you ask a classmate for help instead of the teacher?	❏	❏	❏	❏
6. Do you call the teacher on the telephone?	❏	❏	❏	❏

GAME Making New Friends

team number

In this episode, Rebecca makes a new friend in one of her music classes. How well do you know the people in your class? Play this game to learn more about your classmates and which of them might become good friends of yours.

Get Ready to Play

Step One
Divide the class into two teams. Sit with your teammates while you set up for the game.

Step Two
Each teammate must write a short paragraph about him or herself. You can use any of the topics in the box below for ideas. Try to write about things that your other classmates might not know about you. Use the space on page 6 to write your paragraph. Do not include your name in the paragraph.

Here is a paragraph that Rebecca might have written:

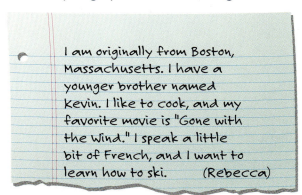

Step Three
Exchange paragraphs with another person on your team. Read each other's paragraphs and help each other fix any mistakes. Copy your new paragraph onto a separate sheet of paper. Now you can write your name at the bottom of your paper, so your teammates will know whose it is.

Step Four
Put all of your teammates' papers into a pile. You're ready to play!

Play the Game

- One person on your team chooses a paragraph from the pile and reads it out loud.
- The other team will try to guess who wrote the paragraph. They may discuss their ideas first before they make a guess.
- If the guess is correct, the team receives one point. If the guess is wrong, the team doesn't get a point. Don't tell the other team the correct answer.
- Teams should take turns reading and guessing. People on the same team should take turns reading the paragraphs out loud to the other team.
- Keep track of your team's correct guesses and points in the charts on page 6.
- When all of the paragraphs have been read, the team with the most points wins.

EPISODE 16 PAGE 5

GAME Making New Friends

Write your first paragraph here. When you're finished, show it to another teammate who will help you fix any mistakes.

_____
_____
_____
_____
_____
_____
_____
_____
_____
_____
_____
_____
_____
_____
_____
_____
_____
_____
_____
_____
_____
_____

Keep track of the points that your team gets here.

Keep track of your team's correct guesses here.

Points for correct guesses	Names that your team has correctly guessed
	_____ _____
	_____ _____
	_____ _____
	_____ _____
	_____ _____
	_____ _____
	_____ _____
	_____ _____

What About You?

1. Is it easy for you to make new friends?
2. Where do you meet new friends?
3. How did you meet your newest friend?

EPISODE **16**   PAGE **6**

Casey at the Bat

EPISODE 17

THEMES
- Sending and Receiving Flowers
- Filling Out Forms
- *Casey at the Bat*, a Famous Poem

INFORMATION GAP
- Spelling

OPTIONAL PROJECT
- Poetry (Appendix 5)

THEME Sending and Receiving Flowers

1 PARTNER DISCUSSION

_____
partner's name

In this episode, Rebecca gets flowers from Alberto. The card with the flowers says, "Save Saturday for me! Something big is happening." Alberto sends flowers to Rebecca as a sign of friendship.

In my country, people send flowers for...
- retirements
- birthdays
- graduations
- funerals
- good luck
- new jobs

A. When do people send flowers in your country? Circle the occasions in the picture above. In the empty spaces, write in three other times when people send flowers.

B. Compare your picture with that of a partner. Do you have different answers? If you do, ask this question: *Why do/don't you send flowers for <u>birthdays</u>?*

C. Ask your partner if there are special flowers for each occasion. Find out what they are. For example, in the United States and Canada, many people send red roses for Valentine's Day.

EPISODE 17 PAGE 1

2 PARTNER OPINIONS

partner's name

What do you think about sending or receiving flowers?

A. Read the sentences below. Put a check (✔) next to the sentences that you *agree* with.

B. Tell your partner the sentences that you agree with. Explain your answers.

C. Now listen to your partner. Check (✔) the sentences your partner agrees with. Make sure your partner explains his/her answers.

	You	Your partner
1. Flowers are only for special occasions.	❏	❏
2. Only men send flowers.	❏	❏
3. It is OK to buy flowers for yourself.	❏	❏
4. A gift of flowers says "Love."	❏	❏

1. Do you like to receive flowers?
2. What is your favorite type of flower?
3. Have you ever sent flowers to someone?

THEME Filling Out Forms

3 GROUP SURVEY

group number

In this episode, Emma Washington gives Rebecca some forms to fill out. Do you have experience filling out forms?

A. Check (✔) the kinds of forms you have filled out.

B. Divide into groups of three people. Ask your group members the question: *Have you ever filled out a medical form?* Check (✔) their answers.

C. If you can, add your own kind of form in number 8.

Have you ever filled out...	You Yes	No	Group member 1 Yes	No	Group member 2 Yes	No
1. a medical form?						
2. an employment application?						
3. a tax form?						
4. a passport application?						
5. a credit card application?						
6. a car rental form?						
7. a college application?						
8. _____ (one more kind of form)						

D. In your opinion, which kind of form is the easiest to fill out? _____

Which kind of form is the most difficult to fill out? _____

4 CLASS BRAINSTORM

Choose two of the forms listed in the chart in Activity 3. As a class, create a list of the kinds of information that you might have to give on each form. Write all of the ideas in the boxes below. Have a student from your class write a "master list" on the board.

EXAMPLE

Form A medical form
Kinds of information
name   age
weight   weight

Form _____
Kinds of information

Form _____
Kinds of information

EPISODE 17 PAGE 3

THEME Casey at the Bat

5 GROUP STORY

group number

Casey at the Bat is a famous poem about baseball, written in 1888. The sentences below tell the story about the poem, but they're not in the right order.

A. With your group, decide on the best order for the sentences. Number them 1 to 12.

B. Read your story to another group. Compare them. Is your story the same as or different from the other group's?

____ a. Casey lets the second pitch go by.
____ b. The game is in Mudville.
____ c. Then "Mighty Casey" comes to bat and the fans cheer.
__1__ d. *Casey at the Bat* is about a baseball game.
____ e. The Mudville team is losing.
____ f. The umpire yells, "Strike two!" and the fans yell, "Kill the umpire!"
____ g. He is sure he will get a big hit.
____ h. "Mighty Casey" has struck out.
____ i. The umpire yells, "Strike one!" and the fans go crazy.
____ j. Casey smiles and quiets the fans.
____ k. Casey lets the first pitch go by.
____ l. On the third pitch he swings and misses.

6 TEAM GAME Time: 10 min.

team number

Below are some words that the poet used to make rhymes in *Casey at the Bat*. With your team, think of words that rhyme with these words. Add them to the lists. The team with the most rhyming words wins.

bat	day	there	place	flew	game	ball	bright
that	play	air	case	two			
sat	say						

1. Do you like to read poems?
2. Can you say any poems from memory?
3. Do you like to write poems?

EPISODE **17** PAGE **4**

INFORMATION GAP Spelling

7 PARTNER — INFORMATION GAP

STUDENT A Work with a partner. One of you works on this page. The other works on page 6. Don't look at your partner's page!

_____
partner's name

In this episode, Rebecca helps Alex study for a spelling test. Are you a good speller? Are spelling rules easy for you to remember?

A. Look at the sentences under A. Read them aloud. Are the missing letters *ie* or *ei*? You decide. Follow the rule in the spelling rhyme. Check your spelling with your partner.
B. Listen to your partner and write the sentences under B.
C. If you need to, ask: "How do you spell…?"

Here is a spelling rule that rhymes:

> **A Spelling Rhyme**
> Write *i* before *e*
> Except after *c*
> Or when sounded like *ay*
> As in *neighbor* and *weigh*.

A

1. One plus seven makes ____ght.
2. Have a p____ce of pizza.
3. Can you touch the c____ling?
4. She's the ch____f of police.

B

1. _____ receive _____?
2. _____ believe _____!
3. _____ field.
4. _____ neighbor.

8 PARTNER — PUZZLE

This crossword puzzle has six pairs of words that sound the same, but are spelled differently. These words are called **homonyms**. Two examples are *see* and *sea*, and *by* and *buy*.

A. Use the clues to write the words that go ACROSS in the puzzle. Say each number and clue to your partner.
B. Listen to your partner's clues. Write the words that go DOWN in the puzzle.
C. Compare puzzles with your partner. Write the six pairs of homonyms on the lines below.

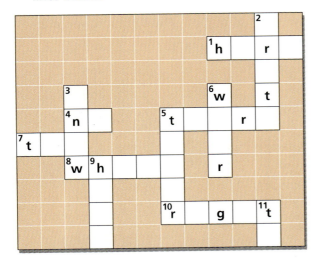

Clues—Across

1. I don't want to go there. I want to stay ____.
4. What is your answer? Yes or ____?
5. ____ are seven days in a week.
7. You eat ____ much food. You are fat.
8. ____ do you live?
10. I am ____, you are wrong.

The six homonyms are:

a. _____ and _____
b. _____ and _____
c. _____ and _____
d. _____ and _____
e. _____ and _____
f. _____ and _____

EPISODE **17**   PAGE **5**

INFORMATION GAP Spelling

7 PARTNER | INFORMATION GAP

STUDENT B Work with a partner. One of you works on this page. The other works on page 5. Don't look at your partner's page!

_____
partner's name

In this episode, Rebecca helps Alex study for a spelling test. Are you a good speller? Are spelling rules easy for you to remember?

A. Listen to your partner and write the sentences under A.
B. Look at the sentences under B. Read them aloud. Are the missing letters *ie* or *ei*? You decide. Follow the rule in the spelling rhyme. Check your spelling with your partner.
C. If you need to, ask: "How do you spell…?"

Here is a spelling rule that rhymes:

> **A Spelling Rhyme**
> Write *i* before *e*
> Except after *c*
> Or when sounded like *ay*
> As in *neighbor* and *weigh*.

A

1. _____ eight.
2. _____ piece _____.
3. _____ ceiling?
4. _____ chief _____.

B

1. Did you rec____ve my letter?
2. I don't bel____ve it!
3. The baseball team is in the f____ld.
4. He's a good n____ghbor.

8 PARTNER | PUZZLE

This crossword puzzle has six pairs of words that sound the same, but are spelled differently. These words are called **homonyms**. Two examples are *see* and *sea*, and *by* and *buy*.

A. Use the clues to write the words that go DOWN in the puzzle. Say each number and clue to your partner.
B. Listen to your partner's clues. Write the words that go ACROSS in the puzzle.
C. Compare puzzles with your partner. Write the six pairs of homonyms on the lines below.

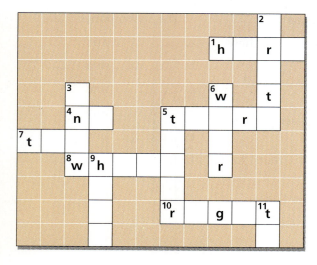

Clues—Down

2. I like to _____ with a pen.
3. Do you _____ how to spell it?
5. They should wash _____ hands.
6. I _____ a sweater if I am cold.
9. Please speak loudly—I can't _____ you.
11. Students go _____ school.

The six homonyms are:

a. _____ and _____
b. _____ and _____
c. _____ and _____
d. _____ and _____
e. _____ and _____
f. _____ and _____

EPISODE **17** PAGE **6**

The Art Gallery

EPISODE 18

THEMES
- Titles of Art Work
- Appreciating Art
- Money vs. Love

GAME
- Selling Something of Value

OPTIONAL PROJECT
- Going to an Art Gallery (Appendix 6)

THEME Titles of Art Work

1 PARTNER GIVING TITLES

_____
partner's name

Alberto calls his photograph of Rebecca "Dream Catcher." With a partner, decide on the best titles for the photographs below. There is one extra title to choose from, but you can use each title only once. Write the titles on the lines underneath the photographs. There are no right or wrong answers!

EXAMPLE Ask this question: *Which is the best title for picture ?*
Explain your ideas: *I think "Good Old Days" is the best title for picture because...*

| Family Values | That's What Friends Are For | At Home | Good Old Days | Dreams |

a. _____   b. _____

c. _____   d. _____

EPISODE **18**   PAGE **1**

2 PARTNER DISCUSSION

partner's name

A. Choose two of the pictures from Activity 1. With a partner, think of your own titles for them.

Picture ____ : _____   Picture ____ : _____

B. Find another pair of students who chose one of your pictures. Compare your titles. Ask this question: *Why did you give it that title?* Repeat this activity with the other picture.

THEME Appreciating Art

3 PARTNER WAYS TO SAY IT

partner's name

Rebecca and Alberto talk about the photographs at the gallery. They use expressions like: "*Some of them are quite good,*" and, "*I especially like this one.*" Here are some other ways to talk about your feelings about art.

| It makes me feel good (happy, upset, nervous). | I like it/I don't like it. | It's very beautiful (funny, ugly). | It bothers me. | It relaxes me. |

Look at the paintings below. Take turns asking your partner about the paintings. Use the expressions above or some of your own.

EXAMPLE

Student A: *What do you think of painting a?*

Student B: *It relaxes me.*

Do you and your partner have the same feelings about any of the paintings? Which ones? _____

EPISODE 18   PAGE 2

4 GROUP — OPINION SURVEY

group number

Which painting from Activity 3 is your favorite?

A. Write a **1** next to the letter of the painting that you like the most. Write a **4** next to the letter of the painting that you like the least. Rate the rest of the paintings in order from 1 to 4.

B. Divide into groups and compare your ratings. Ask your group members this question: *Which painting did you rate number __1__?* Fill in the chart below.

Name	Ratings			
Painting	a	b	c	d
You				
Group member 1				
Group member 2				
Group member 3				

C. Answer these questions with your group:
- *Which painting did most people rate number 1?* _____
- *Which painting did most people rate number 4?* _____
- *Ask each of your group members: Why do you like painting __b__ the most/least?*

THEME Money vs. Love

5 GROUP — DISCUSSION

group number

In this episode, the Mendozas discuss their family business. Their decisions have to do with both feelings and money.

A. What is more important to you—feelings or money? Read each of the situations below, and check (✔) **F** for feelings or **M** for money.

B. Divide into groups. Count the number of **F** and **M** answers for each situation. Write the numbers in the chart.

C. For each situation, which is more important to the group—feelings or money? Discuss the answers.

Situations	You F	You M	Number of ✔s (Group) F	Number of ✔s (Group) M
1. changing a job				
2. getting married				
3. choosing a house to buy				
4. choosing a house to rent				
5. moving to another country				
6. choosing a present for a friend				
7. having children				
8. choosing a college/university				

EPISODE **18** PAGE **3**

6 GROUP   ROLE-PLAY

_____
group number

Your group will pretend to be the Mendoza family. You will talk about whether or not to sell the family restaurant.

A. Divide into groups of four. Decide which member of the family each of you will play. Choose *Mr. Mendoza, Mrs. Mendoza, Ramón,* or *Alberto.*

B. Before you begin, complete this activity with your group.
- Decide if each person wants to sell or keep the restaurant.
- Decide if each person makes this decision because of money or feelings. Circle your answers.

Mr. Mendoza	sell/keep/undecided	money/feelings
Mrs. Mendoza	sell/keep/undecided	money/feelings
Ramón	sell/keep/undecided	money/feelings
Alberto	sell/keep/undecided	money/feelings

C. Now you're ready to role-play. You're a member of the Mendoza family. You're at a family meeting. Say what you think about selling the restaurant. Use the phrases in the box and your own words. Start by asking the other family members questions like:
- *How do you feel about selling the restaurant?*
- *Why do you/don't you want to sell it?*

I agree with _____ because...

I don't agree with _____ because...

The restaurant is my life.

I love this restaurant.

What do we need so much money for?

We/I/you need the money for...

Without the restaurant, what would we do?

Would we be happy without the restaurant?

The restaurant belongs to us.

We could buy another restaurant.

1. Do you worry a lot about money?
2. What was the last decision you made for money?
3. What was the last decision you made for love?
4. Which makes you happier, love or money?

EPISODE **18** PAGE **4**

GAME Selling Something of Value

7 | TEAM | GAME |

team number

In this episode, the Mendoza family talks about selling their restaurant. Play this game about selling something of value. To win, your team must be the first to guess what the other team is selling. You can only ask questions that have **Yes** or **No** for an answer.

Get Ready to Play

Step One
Divide into an even number of teams. Decide which team you will play against.

Step Two
With your teammates, choose an item to sell from the list at the top of page 6.

Step Three
On a piece of paper, write down the item that you are going to sell and its price range. (*Example: the sports car—$50,000–$80,000*)

Step Four
Use the rest of the paper to write down what you find out about the other team's item.

Step Five
Cut out and fold the die on Appendix 13. Cut out a different marker for each team.

Play the Game
- Put your markers on START. Decide which team goes first.
- Roll the die. Move the number of spaces shown.
- Follow the directions on the space where you land.
- If you land on a Question space, ask the other team a *Yes/No* question about the item. Questions can be about size, price range, use, and so on. Questions can't be about the category or name of the item unless you are ready to guess what it is.

  EXAMPLE   RIGHT: Q: Could it cost more than $60,000? (A: Yes.)
                                 Q: Can you wear it? (A: No.)
                     WRONG: Q: Is it jewelry?
                                   Q: Is it a business?

- Remember to write down what you find out about the other team's item. This information will help you ask better questions. Use the list of items for sale as ideas for questions.
- If you land on **Go to the Bank,** you must stay there until you roll a 3 or a 6. When you leave the Bank, go back to **START.**
- If you land on a space that tells you to move **Forward** or **Back,** go to that space and follow the directions there.
- If you land on a **FREE** space, stay there. Wait until your next turn.
- If it is your turn, and you know what the other team is selling, you can make a guess. Be careful! If your guess is wrong, your team loses the game.

EPISODE **18**   PAGE **5**

GAME Selling Something of Value

REAL ESTATE
house: $70,000–$120,000
business: $100,000–$300,000
farm: $50,000–$200,000

CARS
sports car: $50,000–$80,000
used Honda: $10,000–$30,000
1995 Ford: $800–$2,000

FURNITURE
leather couch: $500–$1,000
antique desk: $7,000–$15,000
bookshelf: $700–$3,000

ART
small Picasso painting: $100,000–$300,000
painting by local artist: $500–$1,000
sculpture: $10,000–$30,000

JEWELRY
diamond necklace: $10,000–$30,000
gold watch: $7,000–$15,000
pearl earrings: $500–$2,500

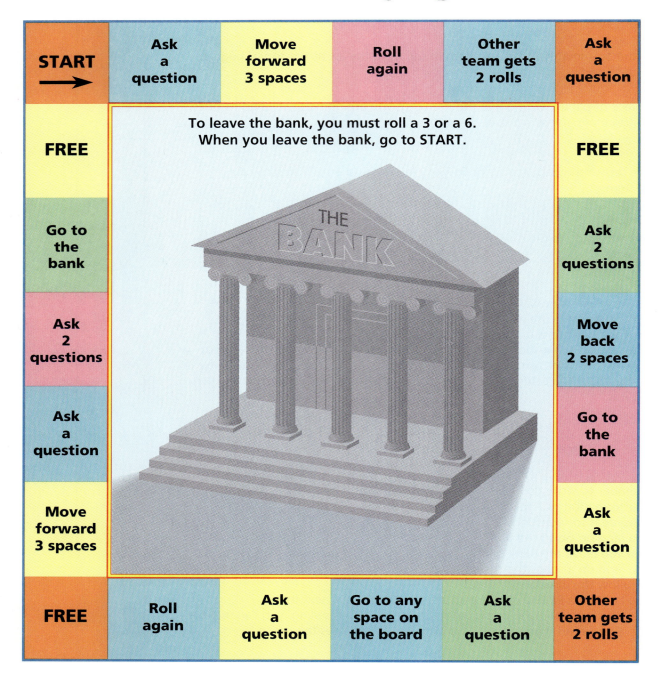

EPISODE **18**   PAGE **6**

The Picnic

EPISODE 19

THEMES
- Having Fun
- Bad Behavior
- Going on a Picnic

INFORMATION GAP
- Getting Close to Someone

OPTIONAL PROJECT
- Team Games (Appendix 7)

THEME Having Fun

1 PARTNER INTERVIEW _____
partner's name

playing sports

watching TV

dancing

having a picnic

reading

going to the movies

playing computer games

hiking

talking with friends

listening to music

Look at the activities above. Circle five activities that are fun for you. Write them below. Then ask your partner this question: *What activities are fun for you?* Write your partner's answers.

Five things that are fun for you
1. _____
2. _____
3. _____
4. _____
5. _____

Five things that are fun for your partner
1. _____
2. _____
3. _____
4. _____
5. _____

EPISODE **19** PAGE **1**

PARTNER   OPINION SURVEY

partner's name

People everywhere have fun in different ways. How do you have fun?

A. Read the four questions below and write your answers in the chart.

B. Divide into groups of four. Then, interview the people in your group. Write their answers in the chart. Which activity from page 1 is the most popular?

	1. Do you have more fun indoors or outdoors? (Check ✔) your answer.		2. Do you have more fun talking or listening? (Check ✔) your answer.		3. Do you have more fun with other people or alone? (Check ✔) your answer.		4. Which activity from page 1 is your favorite? Write it below.
Name	Indoors	Outdoors	Talking	Listening	With others	Alone	Your favorite activity
1. You							
2.							
3.							
4.							

THEME Bad Behavior

 **PARTNER**   INTERVIEW

partner's name

In this episode, two boys behave badly. They steal food from the picnic and they make trouble with Vincent. What is bad behavior?

A. Look at the list below and rate the behaviors from 1 to 8. Write a *1* next to the worst behavior, a *2* next to the second worst behavior, and so on.

B. Ask your partner these questions:
- What behavior is number *1* on your list? Why?
- What behavior is number *8* on your list? Why? Write your partner's answers in the box on the right.

C. Compare the remaining answers with your partner. Are any of them the same? What are they?

YOUR ANSWERS	
Behaviors	**Rating**
calling someone bad names	
cheating on your taxes	
not returning something a friend lets you borrow	
lying to your boss	
stealing something from a store	
gossiping about friends	
littering	
laughing at someone	

Your partner's number 1 answer

_____

Your partner's number 8 answer

_____

EPISODE **19**   PAGE **2**

GROUP DISCUSSION

group number

Divide into groups. Look at the list of bad behaviors in Activity 3. What do you think should happen to people who do these things?

A. Choose *five* of the behaviors from Activity 3 and write them in the chart below.

B. With your group, discuss an appropriate consequence (something that should happen) for each of these behaviors. Write all of your ideas on a separate piece of paper, and then put your final ideas in the chart below.

C. As a class, compare your answers with those of other groups. Do you have similar answers for certain behaviors?

Behavior	What should happen (consequence)
EXAMPLE littering	If someone litters, he or she should spend a Saturday afternoon cleaning the streets of the neighborhood.
1.	
2.	
3.	
4.	
5.	

1. How did your parents punish you when you behaved badly as a child?
2. What is the worst punishment you ever got for bad behavior?
3. Have you ever punished someone for bad behavior? What did you do?

THEME Going on a Picnic

5   TEAM   GAME   Time: 10 min.

_____
team number

Going on a picnic is a popular activity in the United States and Canada. People go on picnics with their family and friends. Sometimes schools, churches, companies, and other groups have special picnics. Parks and beaches are popular picnic places.

Look at the picnic scene below. With your teammates, write as many words as you can for each of the categories below. Some words are in the picture to help you, but you can also add any words of your own. The team with the most correct answers wins.

Things that people are eating or drinking

_____ _____ _____ _____ _____
_____ _____ _____ _____ _____

Things that people are using

_____ _____ _____ _____ _____
_____ _____ _____ _____ _____

Things that people are doing

_____ _____ _____ _____ _____
_____ _____ _____ _____ _____

1. Do you remember a picnic that you went on? Who did you go with?
2. What kinds of food did you have?
3. What is the best place for a picnic where you live?

EPISODE **19** PAGE **4**

INFORMATION GAP Getting Close to Someone

6 PARTNER INFORMATION GAP

STUDENT A Work with a partner. One of you works on this page. The other works on page 6. Don't look at your partner's page.

_____
partner's name

In this episode, Rebecca and Ramón are "getting close"—they're becoming better friends as they talk together and learn more about each other. In the United States and Canada, it's common to talk about personal things with a new friend if both people are comfortable.

Imagine that Rebecca and Ramón's conversation at the picnic continues.

Part One

Read what Rebecca tells Ramón. Then, answer your partner's questions about Rebecca. Your partner will write down your answers. When your partner has finished, read the conversation below out loud so that your partner can check his/her answers.

> Ramón: So, what do you do in your spare time besides go to school and work at the after-school program?
> Rebecca: Well, I really love to go to the movies—comedies are my favorite. And I love going out to eat.
> Ramón: Me too! What's your favorite kind of food?
> Rebecca: I especially like Italian food. Pizza, spaghetti—all of it!
> Ramón: How about those Italian deserts?
> Rebecca: No, I don't eat them. I don't like sweets very much.
> Ramón: What do you like to do on Saturdays when you're not at a picnic?
> Rebecca: Let's see...I always try to exercise in the morning. I like to start my day with a walk or a bike ride. Sometimes I cook dinner for my roommates. I'm a pretty good cook—I have a lot of practice!

Part Two

Ask your partner the following questions about what Ramón tells Rebecca. Write down what your partner tells you. Then listen as your partner reads you the conversation between Rebecca and Ramón. Check your answers.

1. What does Ramón usually do on Saturdays? _____
2. What sport does he like to play? _____
3. What does he like to read? _____
4. Where does Ramón go on vacation? _____
5. Who does he take with him? _____

EPISODE **19**   PAGE **5**

INFORMATION GAP Getting Close to Someone

6 PARTNER INFORMATION GAP

STUDENT B Work with a partner. One of you works on this page. The other works on page 5. Don't look at your partner's page.

_____
partner's name

In this episode, Rebecca and Ramón are "getting close"—they're becoming better friends as they talk together and learn more about each other. In the United States and Canada, it's common to talk about personal things with a new friend if both people are comfortable.

Imagine that Rebecca and Ramón's conversation at the picnic continues.

Part One

Ask your partner the following questions about what Rebecca tells Ramón. Write down what your partner tells you. Then listen as your partner reads you the conversation between Rebecca and Ramón. Check your answers.

1. What kind of movies does Rebecca like to see?
2. What's her favorite kind of food?
3. What doesn't Rebecca do?
4. What does she always do on Saturdays?
5. What does Rebecca say she is good at?

Part Two

Read what Ramón tells Rebecca. Then, answer your partner's questions about what Ramón says. Your partner will write down your answers. When your partner has finished, read the conversation below out loud so that your partner can check his/her answers.

Rebecca: How about you? What do you usually do on Saturdays?
Ramón: Well, Saturday is a very busy day at the restaurant, so I usually have to work. But sometimes, Alex and I play a little soccer before I have to go to the restaurant.
Rebecca: Is soccer your favorite sport?
Ramón: I enjoy watching soccer, but I like to play tennis more.
Rebecca: What else do you enjoy doing?
Ramón: When I have the time, I really love to read—all kinds of things, but mostly novels. It's too bad that I work so much—I'd like to have more time to read.
Rebecca: Do you ever take a vacation from work and go away?
Ramón: Yes. I take a vacation about once a year. I usually try to go to the mountains with my father and Alex.

EPISODE **19**   PAGE **6**

Prejudice

EPISODE 20

THEMES
- Apologizing
- Teaching Children Right from Wrong
- Appreciating Differences

INFORMATION GAP
- Prejudice in the U.S.

OPTIONAL PROJECT
- Greeting Cards (Appendix 8)

THEME Apologizing

1 PARTNER — WAYS TO SAY IT

_____
partner's name

In this episode, a girl writes an apology to Vincent. She's sorry she laughed at him. Here are some ways people apologize in English:

I'm sorry.	I apologize.	Please forgive me.
I'm sorry about laughing.	I apologize for saying that.	It was wrong of me to laugh.
I'm sorry that I did that.	Please accept my apologies for being late.	

Work with a partner. Look at the situations below. Take turns. One person chooses a situation. The other person chooses an expression for an apology. Then, make up your own situation.

Situations

EXAMPLE   You forgot your friend's birthday.

1. You said something that hurt your friend's feelings.
2. You spilled something on your classmate's new shirt.
3. You forgot to call your mother.
4. You lied to a close friend.
5. You didn't finish the work your boss gave you.
6. Your situation:

Expressions

I apologize for forgetting your birthday.

_____
_____
_____
_____
_____
_____

1. Can you remember making an apology to someone?
2. Is it easy for you to apologize to someone?
3. Did anyone ever refuse to accept your apology?
4. When do you feel that you don't have to apologize?

THEME Teaching Children Right from Wrong

2 GROUP RANKING

group number

How do children learn right from wrong?

A. Rank the items below from 1 to 7, with 1 as the most important and 7 as the least important.

B. Read your list to your group members. They will write down your answers.

C. Now listen to your group members read their lists. Write their answers in the chart below. Compare and discuss your answers.

Children learn right from wrong...	You	Group member 1	Group member 2	Group member 3
from experience.				
by listening to their parents.				
by watching their parents.				
from their teachers in school.				
from formal religious education.				
from their friends.				

3 PARTNER MATCHING

partner's name

Below are some famous proverbs that have to do with teaching children right from wrong.

A. With your partner, match the proverbs and their meanings.

B. With the people in your group, decide on the proverb that offers the best advice about teaching children.

The proverb with the best advice is number _____.

1. *Practice what you preach.*

2. *Actions speak louder than words.*

3. *Do as I say, not as I do.*

4. *Children should be seen and not heard.*

5. *Spare the rod and spoil the child.*

____ a. Don't do the same things I do. Do what I tell you to do.

____ b. If you don't punish your children, they'll grow up badly.

____ c. You should live the way you tell other people to live.

____ d. Children should not say anything around adults.

____ e. What you do is more important than what you say.

C. Is there a proverb in your own language that is similar to any of these? Share the proverb with your class and explain its meaning.

EPISODE 20 PAGE 2

THEME Appreciating Differences

4 GROUP SURVEY

group number

Are you very different from the people in your group? Let's find out!

A. Divide into groups of four students. In your group, choose a partner. This person is Group member 1.

B. With this partner, decide on *two* ways that you are different and *one* way that you are the same. Complete the sentences below for Group member 1.

C. Change partners in your group. Find ways that you and this next group member are different and the same. Complete the sentences for Group member 2.

D. Work with Group member 3, the last person in your group. Complete the sentences below for Group member 3.

EXAMPLE I come from Mexico but Takako comes from Japan .
         I have a sister but Takako only has a brother .
         We both can play the piano .

Group member 1:

I _____ but _____ .
I _____ but _____ .
We both _____ .

Group member 2:

I _____ but _____ .
I _____ but _____ .
We both _____ .

Group member 3:

I _____ but _____ .
I _____ but _____ .
We both _____ .

5 GROUP DISCUSSION

group number

What kinds of things make you and your group members different from each other? What things make you alike?

A. Compare your answers from Activity 2.

B. On a separate sheet of paper, make a list that contains the kinds of similarities and differences that your group found.

EXAMPLE   Similarities   Differences
          ability to play the piano   home country

EPISODE **20** PAGE **3**

GROUP DISCUSSION

_____
group number

How do you feel about differences among people? Check (✔) your responses to the following statements. Then form a group. Ask volunteers to share their reasons for their answers.

	I agree	I disagree
1. I sometimes feel different from other people.	_____	_____
2. It feels good to be different.	_____	_____
3. It can be dangerous to be different from others.	_____	_____
4. People usually respect differences in others.	_____	_____
5. People are really all the same.	_____	_____

THEME Prejudice in the U.S.

 GROUP DISCUSSION

_____
group number

In the United States, many people have experienced prejudice. Sometimes there's violence, sometimes there isn't.

A. Think about your own country. Maybe you have read in the newspaper about people experiencing prejudice. Maybe you have seen someone suffer from prejudice. Or maybe you have experienced it yourself.
B. Read the questions in the chart below and check (✔) your answers.
C. Form a group and share your experiences. Compare your answers. Ask the people in your group these questions:
- *What kind of examples can you give?*
- *How did it make you feel?*
- *Is there anything you can do to change the situation?*

In your country, is there...	No.	I'm not sure.	Yes. I've read about it.	Yes. I've seen it.	Yes. I've experienced it.
1. prejudice based on race?					
2. prejudice against people from other countries?					
3. prejudice based on age?					
4. prejudice against people with disabilities?					
5. _____ (another type of prejudice)					

EPISODE 20   PAGE 4

INFORMATION GAP Prejudice in the U.S.

8 PARTNER   INFORMATION GAP

_____
partner's name

STUDENT A Work with a partner. One of you works on this page. The other works on page 6. Don't look at your partner's page.

Below is your half of a secret message. It's part of a famous speech about prejudice in the United States. You'll need to use the code to figure it out.

A. Work with your partner to complete the code. Ask the question: *What letter does 3 stand for?*
B. Once you know the code, write down all of the words on your page.
C. Your partner has the words that appear as X's. Figure out the message together.

Code

1 =	4 = S	7 = M	10 = A	13 = W	16 =	19 =	22 = I	25 = Y
2 = E	5 =	8 =	11 =	14 = G	17 =	20 = Q	23 =	26 =
3 =	6 = C	9 =	12 =	15 = U	18 = K	21 =	24 = O	

"22   X X X X   10   1 8 2 10 7   X X X X   7 25   X X X X   5 22 9 9 5 2
" I ____ ___ _____ ____ __ ____ _____

X X X X X X X X   13 22 5 5   X X X   1 10 25   X X X X   22 3   10
_____ _____ ___ ___ ____ __ _

X X X X X X   13 11 2 8 2   X X X X   13 22 5 5   X X X   12 2
_____ _____ ____ _____ ___ __

X X X X X X   12 25 9 11 2   X X X X X   24 16 9 11 2 22 8   X X X X
_____ _____ _____ _____ ____

12 15 9   X X   X X X   6 24 3 9 2 3 9   X X   X X X X X
___ __ ___ _____ __ _____

6 11 10 8 10 6 9 2 8"
_____."

These words were spoken by a famous American. He was a civil rights leader. He said these words on August 28, 1963 in Washington, D.C. In 1964 he won the Nobel Peace Prize. He was shot and killed on April 4, 1968.

Work with your partner to fill in the other letters of his name.

M _ R _ I _   _ U _ H _ R K _ N _ ,   _ R.

INFORMATION GAP Prejudice in the U.S.

8 PARTNER INFORMATION GAP

STUDENT **B** Work with a partner. One of you works on this page. The other works on page 5. Don't look at your partner's page.

_____
partner's name

Below is your half of a secret message. It's part of a famous speech about prejudice in the United States. You'll need to use the code to figure it out.

A. Work with your partner to complete the code. Ask the question: *What letter does 2 stand for?*

B. Once you know the code, write down all of the words on your page.

C. Your partner has the words that appear as X's. Figure out the message together.

Code

1 = D	4 =	7 =	10 =	13 =	16 = F	19 = J	22 =	25 =
2 =	5 = L	8 = R	11 = H	14 =	17 = P	20 =	23 = Z	26 = V
3 = N	6 =	9 = T	12 = B	15 =	18 =	21 = X	24 =	

"X 11 10 26 2 X X X X X X 9 11 10 9 X X 16 24 15 8 X X X X X X
"___ H A V E ___ _____ _____ ___ _____ _____

6 11 22 5 1 8 2 3 X X X X 24 3 2 X X X 5 22 26 2 X X X
_____ ____ _____ _____ ___ ___

3 10 9 22 24 3 X X X X X 9 11 2 25 X X X X 3 24 9 X X
_____ _____ _____ _____ _____ ___

19 15 1 14 2 1 X X X X X 6 24 5 24 8 X X X X X X X 4 18 22 3
_____ __ ___ _____ __ _____ _____

X X X 12 25 9 11 2 X X X X X X X 24 16 9 11 2 22 8
___ __ ___ _____ ___ _____

X X X X X X X X"
_____."

These words were spoken by a famous American. He was a civil rights leader. He said these words on August 28, 1963 in Washington, D.C. In 1964 he won the Nobel Peace Prize. He was shot and killed on April 4, 1968.

Work with your partner to fill in the other letters of his name.

_ A _ T _ N   L _ T _ E _   _ I _ G, J _ .

EPISODE 20 PAGE 6

A Difficult Decision

EPISODE 21

THEMES
- A Daily Schedule
- Being Stubborn
- Missing a Friend

GAME
- Solving Problems

OPTIONAL PROJECT
- Making Decisions (Appendix 9)

THEME A Daily Schedule

1 PARTNER INTERVIEW

_____
partner's name

In this episode, Rebecca has a very busy day. She goes to class, studies in the library, and works at the after-school program. What's your daily schedule?

A. Think about a typical day in your life. What do you usually do? Write down your activities in the schedule below.

B. Ask your partner about his/her schedule. Ask the question: *What do you usually do from 6:00 a.m. to 9:00 a.m.?* Write your partner's answers.

You	Schedule	Your partner
EXAMPLE I read the paper during breakfast. I leave for work at 6:30.	6:00 a.m.–9:00 a.m.	He makes breakfast for his family. He exercises before he goes to work.
	6:00 a.m.–9:00 a.m.	
	9:00 a.m.–12:00 p.m.	
	12.00 p.m.–3:00 p.m.	
	3:00 p.m.–6:00 p.m.	
	6:00 p.m.–9:00 p.m.	
	9:00 p.m.–12:00 a.m.	
	12:00 a.m.–6:00 a.m.	

2 GROUP SURVEY

group number _____

How do you feel about your daily schedule? Is it too busy? Is it just right?

A. Read the sentences below and check (✔) *I agree* or *I disagree*.

B. Divide into groups. Count the number of *agree* and *disagree* answers for each statement. Write the number in the column under GROUP.

	YOU		GROUP (write the number)	
	I agree	I disagree	I agree	I disagree
1. My schedule is too busy.	❑	❑		
2. My schedule is very flexible.	❑	❑		
3. I have a busier schedule than most people I know.	❑	❑		
4. I have a lot of free time.	❑	❑		
5. I don't have enough time to do things that I enjoy.	❑	❑		
6. My schedule is different every day.	❑	❑		
7. I would like to change many things about my schedule.	❑	❑		
8. I am happy with my schedule. I would not like to change it.	❑	❑		

C. Answer the questions below.
- Are most people in your group happy or unhappy with their schedules? _____
- How many people think they are too busy? _____
- Is there anyone in your group who doesn't want to change his/her schedule? Who is it? _____
  Why doesn't he/she want to change it? _____
- Out of the people in your group, who is the happiest about his/her schedule? _____
  Who is the least happy? _____

THEME Being Stubborn

3 CLASS BRAINSTORM

In this episode, Mr. Wang is very stubborn—he doesn't want to change his mind about Vincent and the after-school program. Can you get Mr. Wang to change his mind?

A. Work with your classmates. Think of reasons that Mr. Wang should let Vincent return to the after-school program. Write them on a separate sheet of paper.

B. Ask a classmate or your teacher to write a "master list" on the board for everyone to see.

C. When you're finished, vote on the five best reasons that might convince Mr. Wang to let Vincent return to the program.

4 PARTNER ROLE-PLAY

partner's name

How stubborn are you? Who will give up first? Find out by role-playing with your partner.

A. Choose one of the situations below.
B. Your partner will try to make you change your mind. You're very stubborn. Listen to what your partner says. Tell your partner why you will not change your mind.
C. If you can't think of anything to say in 10 seconds, *your partner* wins.
D. If your partner can't think of anything to say in 10 seconds, *you* win! You are really stubborn!
E. Choose another situation and switch roles. Now you will try to convince your partner to change his or her mind.

Situations

- You're on a long car trip. Your partner wants to stop and get something to eat. You want to keep driving.
- You're looking for a gift for a friend. The store doesn't have anything you like. Your partner is the sales clerk. He/she tries to convince you to buy something anyway.
- Your partner asks to borrow a large amount of money from you. You have the money in the bank, but you don't want to give it to your partner.
- You and your partner are going to the movies. You want to see a comedy. Your partner wants you to go to a horror film.
- You have a new car. Your partner wants to borrow it for the weekend. You don't want your partner to use your car.
- Your situation: _____

1. Do you think you're stubborn?
2. Who's the most stubborn person you know?
3. When someone is very stubborn, how do you get that person to change his/her mind?

EPISODE **21** PAGE **3**

THEME **Missing a Friend**

5 **PARTNER** **SHARING**

_____
partner's name

When Mr. and Mrs. Wang take Vincent out of the after-school program, his classmates miss him. Alex misses Vincent a lot because they're good friends. Who do you miss?

Step One

Ask your partner the questions below. They're about a person your partner misses. Write what your partner says.

1. What's the person's name?	
2. Is she/he a relative or a friend?	
3. Where is this person now?	
4. Why do you miss this person?	
5. When did you see this person last?	
6. When will you see this person again?	
7. What do you like best about him/her?	
8. What is your favorite memory of this person?	
9. Your own question:	

Step Two

On the lines below, write a short paragraph about the person your partner described.

_____
_____
_____
_____
_____
_____

Step Three

When you've finished your paragraph, read what you have written to your partner. Your partner will tell you if you have understood everything correctly.

GAME Solving Problems

6 CLASS GAME

Because Vincent's parents won't let him return to the after-school program, Vincent and Alex won't be able to see each other anymore. Rebecca has an idea for solving the problem. She says: "I'll ask the Wangs if I can give guitar lessons to Vincent and Alex at Vincent's house."

Play this game and help your classmates solve their problems.

Get Ready to Play

Step One
- Work as a class. Read the list of problems in the box on page 6. These are problems that people have in everyday life.
- As a class, add more problems to the list. Think of as many problems as there are students in your class.
- Write the problems in the empty spaces in the box. Use a separate sheet of paper if necessary. Have someone write a "master list" on the board.

Step Two
- Divide into groups. Your teacher will assign each person in your group a different problem from the list on page 6.
- In your group, discuss each problem. Ask people their ideas for solving your problem. Write down your classmates' ideas. Then choose the best solution.
- Cut a piece of paper in half. On one half, write down the problem. On the other half, write down the solution to the problem. Here is an example:

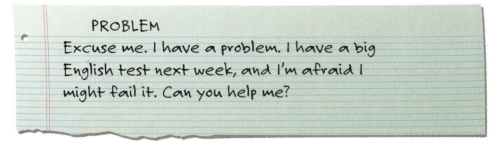

PROBLEM
Excuse me. I have a problem. I have a big English test next week, and I'm afraid I might fail it. Can you help me?

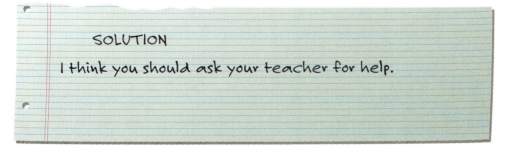

SOLUTION
I think you should ask your teacher for help.

Step Three
- Give all of your cards to your teacher. Your teacher will mix all of the problem cards together into one pile, and the solution cards in another.
- Each student takes one problem card and one solution card.
  IMPORTANT: Make sure your two cards do NOT match. If your solution card matches your problem card, exchange one of the cards with another student.

GAME Solving Problems

 | CLASS | GAME

Play the Game
- Walk around the class and talk to different classmates. Try to find the person who has the solution to your problem.
- Tell a classmate your problem. Your classmate will read you his or her solution card.
- If the person has the correct solution to your problem, take the solution card.
- If the person doesn't have the solution to your problem, he/she will say, "I'm sorry, but I can't help you."
- Keep talking to your classmates until everyone has found the solution to his/her problem. How long did it take your class to solve everyone's problems?

Problems

1. My landlord has raised the rent on my apartment. I can't afford to live there now.
2. I have two children. They're young now, but I want to save money so they can go to college. I don't know what to do.
3. I don't like my boss at work. I work hard, but the boss always criticizes me.
4. I can't decide what subject to major in at school. I like math and science, and I enjoy working with people.
5. I want to stop smoking. I know it's bad for my health, but I don't know how to quit.
6. My parents are getting older. They live in their own apartment now, but soon they won't be able to do this. I'm not sure what to do for them.
7. My girlfriend/boyfriend wants to marry me. I'm not sure if I'm ready to do this. I want to finish school and get a good job first.
8. _____
9. _____
10. _____
11. _____
12. _____
13. _____
14. _____
15. _____
16. _____
17. _____
18. _____
19. _____
20. _____

EPISODE 21   PAGE 6

EPISODE 22

THEMES
- Marriage
- Accepting a Gift
- Children and Homework

INFORMATION GAP
- Favors for Friends

OPTIONAL PROJECT
- Television (Appendix 10)

THEME Marriage

1 GROUP DISCUSSION

_____
group number

In this episode, Alex asks his father if he will ever get married again. What do you think makes for a successful marriage?

A. Look at the items in the chart below. How important is each item in a successful marriage? Write your answers in the chart.

| VI = very important | I = important | NI = not important |

You	For a successful marriage, a husband and wife should…	Group
	enjoy the same hobbies.	
	be the same age.	
	share the same religion.	
	like the same kind of food.	
	have good communication.	
	agree about how to raise children.	
	know each other for a long time before marriage.	
	come from similar family backgrounds.	
	come from the same culture.	

B. Compare answers with the people in your group. For each item, look at everyone's answer and write the *most common* answer in the chart under **Group**.

C. Which answers did you have that were different from those of the rest of the group? Discuss these differences with your group members.

2 CLASS BRAINSTORM

With your classmates, think of more things that make a marriage successful. Write your ideas on a separate piece of paper, and have a classmate or the teacher write a "master list" on the board. How many more things can you think of?

3 GROUP DEBATE

_____
group number

Do you think Ramón should get married again if he falls in love with someone? How will this make Alex feel?

A. Your teacher will divide the class into three groups. Groups 1 and 2 will debate. Group 3 decides the winner of the debate.

B. Read and follow the directions for your group.

Group 1

Your position   *Ramón should definitely get married if he falls in love with someone. It is important for him to be happy in his personal life.*

Talk about the reasons for this position. Write them down.
Prepare to present your reasons.

Group 2

Your position   *Ramón shouldn't get married again. He should just take care of Alex.*

Talk about the reasons for this position. Write them down.
Prepare to present your reasons.

Group 3

During the debate, you can take notes on good ideas. After the debate, choose the winner.

Decide: Which team presented the best ideas?

C. Groups 1 and 2 take turns presenting their positions. Then Group 3 meets to decide which group gave the best presentation. Group 3 announces its decision.

D. The whole class votes on the answer to this question: *Should Ramón get married again?*

1. Who do you know that has a good marriage?
2. What makes their marriage successful?
3. Do you know anyone who is divorced?

THEME Accepting a Gift

4 PARTNER DISCUSSION

partner's name

In this episode, Mrs. Wang gives Rebecca a gift. Rebecca likes the vase, but she doesn't think she should accept it.

When is it appropriate to accept a gift? When shouldn't you accept a gift?

A. Read the following situations and check (✔) *Yes* or *No*.
B. Discuss each situation with your partner and compare answers.
C. If you don't understand your partner's answer, ask this question:
   Why <u>do you/don't you</u> think it is appropriate to accept this gift?
   Ask your partner to explain his/her answers.

Is it appropriate to accept this gift?	You		Your partner	
1. A student gives his/her teacher some money at the end of the semester.	❏ Yes	❏ No	❏ Yes	❏ No
2. An employee gives the boss a desk calendar for his/her birthday.	❏ Yes	❏ No	❏ Yes	❏ No
3. A supervisor (male) gives his secretary (female) an expensive piece of jewelry.	❏ Yes	❏ No	❏ Yes	❏ No
4. A person gives a new neighbor a plant as a welcome gift.	❏ Yes	❏ No	❏ Yes	❏ No
5. A parent gives a 40-year-old son a birthday present.	❏ Yes	❏ No	❏ Yes	❏ No

5 PARTNER WAYS TO SAY IT

partner's name

Rebecca accepts a gift from Mrs. Wang. She says, "Thank you very much." Here are some other ways to accept a gift:

> Thank you. I appreciate it very much.   You shouldn't have!
>
> How thoughtful of you.   What a nice thing to do!

Work with a partner. Look at the situations below. Take turns. One person chooses a situation. The other person chooses an expression to show his/her sympathy. Then, make up your own situation.

	Situations	Expressions
EXAMPLE	Your sister gives you a book you wanted.	How thoughtful of you.
	1. Your boss gives you a pen for your birthday.	
	2. Your friend gives you some flowers.	
	3. Your brother gives you a painting for your new home.	
	4. Your neighbor gives you some freshly baked cookies.	
	5. Your situation:	

THEME Children and Homework

6 CLASS POLL

Alex's grandmother helps him with his homework. How do you feel about children and homework? Do you have the same ideas as your classmates?

A. Circle your answers to the questions below.

1. At what age should children start getting homework?

   a. 5-7 years **b.** 7-9 years **c.** 9-11 years **d.** older than 11

2. How much time should a child Alex's age spend on homework every day?

   a. 1 hour or less **b.** 1-2 hours **c.** 3 hours or more

3. Who is the best person to help a child with homework?

   a. a parent **b.** the child's teacher **c.** a sister or brother **d.** a friend

4. Which statement do you most agree with?

   a. Homework does not help children become better students.

   b. Homework helps children become more responsible.

   c. Homework helps children become better students.

   d. Homework is as important as classroom learning.

B. Your teacher will count the answers for each question above.

- What was the most common answer for question 1? _____
- What was the most common answer for question 2? _____
- What was the most common answer for question 3? _____
- What was the most common answer for question 4? _____

How do your ideas compare with those of your classmates?

7 TEAM GAME Time: 10 min.

_____
team number

How important is homework?

A. Divide into teams. Copy the chart below onto a separate piece of paper. Add more lines.

Reasons that children SHOULD be given homework	Reasons that children SHOULD NOT be given homework
1.	1.
2.	2.

B. With your teammates, write as many reasons as you can to support both ideas in the chart. Start talking and writing when your teacher tells you, and stop when the time is up.

C. Join another team and compare lists. Cross out any reasons that are the same or that are very close. Then, count the reasons that you have left over.

D. The team with the most ideas left wins.

EPISODE 22 PAGE 4

INFORMATION GAP Favors for Friends

8 PARTNER   INFORMATION GAP

STUDENT A Work with a partner. One of you works with this page. The other works on page 6. Don't look at your partner's page!

_____
partner's name

In this episode, you saw many people *doing favors* for others—simple things to help their friends or family. Rebecca offers free guitar lessons to the boys, so that they can see each other. Mrs. Mendoza volunteers to help out while Ramón goes to see his ex-wife. Rebecca does the simple favor of listening to Ramón when he really needs someone to talk to.

In this information gap, you'll have a chance to do a favor for your partner. Will you be able to help?

Part One

A. Your partner will ask you for a favor—and you're willing to help. First, read the information below.

Your situation:
- You have no plans tonight.
- Your child is home with the flu. She's not feeling well.
- You have a car, but you don't know how to drive.
- Your spouse is working.

B. Listen to the favor your partner needs you to do. Can you help? How?

C. If you're not able to do the exact favor your partner wants, think of other ways you can help. You may need to ask your partner some questions.

D. When you agree on a solution, write it on the line below.

How can you help your partner? _____

Part Two

A. You need to ask your partner for a favor. Read the information below and then decide what kind of favor your partner can do for you.

> You have an important meeting at work today that you can't miss. There is a big leak in your ceiling, and the repairman can only come to fix it today. The repairman can come either between 10-12 or between 4-5 in the afternoon.

B. Ask your partner for a favor by saying, *Could you do me a favor?* Explain what your partner can do for you.

C. If your partner can't help you in that way, talk about other things your partner might be able to do for you. You may need to ask your partner some questions.

D. When you agree on a solution, write it on the line below.

How can your partner help you? _____

Part Three

Join another pair from your class, and compare the favors from Part One and Part Two. Do you have similar answers?

EPISODE 22   PAGE 5

INFORMATION GAP Favors for Friends

8 PARTNER INFORMATION GAP
STUDENT B Work with a partner. One of you works with this page. The other works on page 5. Don't look at your partner's page!

_____
partner's name

In this episode, you saw many people *doing favors* for others—simple things to help their friends or family. Rebecca offers free guitar lessons to the boys, so that they can see each other. Mrs. Mendoza volunteers to help out while Ramón goes to see his ex-wife. Rebecca does the simple favor of listening to Ramón when he really needs someone to talk to.

In this information gap, you'll have a chance to do a favor for your partner. Will you be able to help?

Part One

A. You need to ask your partner for a favor. Read the information below and then decide what kind of favor your partner can do for you.

> *Your sister is arriving at the airport late tonight. You're the only one who can pick her up. You car is at the garage for repairs. Your 7 year-old son should be in bed when you have to go to the airport, and your spouse is away on a business trip.*

B. Ask your partner for a favor by saying, *Could you do me a favor?* Explain what your partner can do for you.
C. If your partner can't help you in that way, talk about other things your partner might be able to do for you. You may need to ask your partner some questions.
D. When you agree on a solution, write it on the line below.

How can your partner help you? _____

Part Two

A. Your partner will ask you for a favor—and you're willing to help. First, read the information below.

   Your situation:
   - You have the day off today.
   - You're meeting a friend for lunch. You've cancelled this lunch two times already, and you really don't want to cancel it again.
   - You have to go to the bank.
   - You have to be home by 5:00 to let your dog out.

B. Listen to the favor your partner needs you to do. Can you help? How?
C. If you're not able to do the exact favor your partner wants, think of other ways you can help. You may need to ask your partner some questions.
D. When you agree on a solution, write it on the line below.

How can you help your partner? _____

Part Three

Join another pair from your class, and compare the favors from Part One and Part Two. Do you have similar answers?

EPISODE **22**   PAGE **6**

The Retirement Party

EPISODE 23

THEMES
- Moving Away
- Disciplining Children
- Retirement

GAME
- Gossip

OPTIONAL PROJECT
- International Celebrations (Appendix 11)

THEME Moving Away

1 GROUP DISCUSSION

group number

In this episode, Ramón tells Alex that his mother wants him to move to Los Angeles. Should Alex move? With your group, discuss the reasons that Alex should or should not move. Write your ideas on the lines in the picture below. Add more lines if necessary.

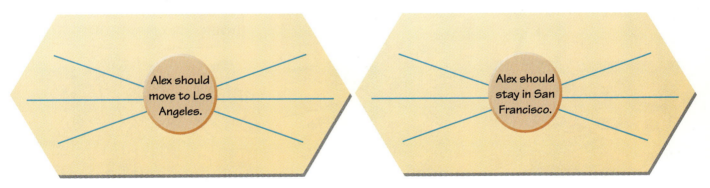

2 CLASS GAME

If you could move anywhere in the world, where would you go? Sit in a circle. One person begins the game by saying, "If I could move anywhere in the world, I would move to **Antarctica**. The word "**Antarctica**" begins with the letter **a**. The next person must think of a place to move that begins with the letter **b**. That person says, "If I could move anywhere in the world, I would move to **Antarctica** or **Brazil**." Each person repeats all the places and adds a new one that starts with the next letter of the alphabet. Keep going until someone forgets a place or until you reach the end of the alphabet. Play another game and try to think of different places.

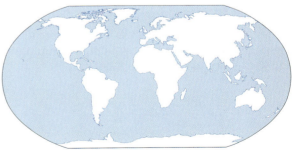

Start with this sentence: If I could move anywhere in the world, I would move to _____

EPISODE **23**   PAGE **1**

3 **PARTNER** **INTERVIEW**

partner's name

Read the questions in the chart below, and complete your answers. Then, ask your partner the questions, and write his/her answers in the chart.

	You	Your partner
1. Have you ever moved?		
2. Would you like to move in the future?		
3. If you could move anywhere in the world, where would you move?		
4. If you moved to a new city tomorrow, what three things would you miss most about the place you live now?	1. 2. 3.	1. 2. 3.

 4 **PARTNER** **STORYTELLING**

partner's name

_____

_____

_____

Work with a partner. Number the pictures in order. Then, make up a story about the person in the pictures. Your story should be about moving to a new place. Tell your story to the entire class.

EPISODE 23   PAGE 2

THEME Disciplining Children

5 PARTNER BRAINSTORM

_____
partner's name

In this episode, Alex and his father have an argument, and Alex tries to run away. Ramón disciplines his son by talking to him. There are many different ways to discipline children.

A. With your partner, think of different ways to discipline children. Write your five best answers below.

1. _____ 4. _____

2. _____ 5. _____

3. _____

B. Discuss what type of discipline should be used in each of these situations. How should a 10-year-old child be disciplined if he/she…

1. steals something from a store? _____

2. gets bad grades in school? _____

3. forgets to do household chores? _____

4. uses bad words (swears)? _____

5. Your situation: _____

6 CLASS DEBATE

How do you feel about physical punishment (spanking)?

A. Read the two opinions below. Put a check (✔) next to the opinion you agree with. Your teacher will divide the class into groups of people who have the same opinion.

B. In your group, make a list of at least five reasons why you believe your opinion is true.

C. Each group will read its list of reasons to the whole class. The rest of the class will ask questions.

D. After all groups have read its reasons, the whole class will vote on the best reason to support each opinion.

_____ *Opinion A:* Sometimes, it is OK to use physical punishment with children.

Reasons

1. _____ 4. _____

2. _____ 5. _____

3. _____

_____ *Opinion B:* It is never OK to use physical punishment with children.

Reasons

1. _____ 4. _____

2. _____ 5. _____

3. _____

EPISODE **23** PAGE **3**

THEME **Retirement**

 PARTNER   INTERVIEW

_____
partner's name

In the United States and Canada, many people retire, or stop working, at age 65. How old do you want to be when you retire? What do you want to do when you retire?

A. Write your answers in the chart below.
B. Ask your partner these questions:
- *How old do you want to be when you retire?*
- *What activities do you want to do when you retire?*

You	Your partner
Your retirement age _____	Your partner's retirement age _____
Activities you want to do when you retire	Activities your partner wants to do when he/she retires
1.	1.
2.	2.
3.	3.
4.	4.
5.	5.

 GROUP   DISCUSSION

_____
group number

Some people believe that there should be laws to force people to retire at age 65. What do you think? Can people continue to work after the age of 65? What kinds of jobs can they do? Discuss this issue with your group. Write your answers below.

Jobs that people can do after 65

1. _____   6. _____
2. _____   7. _____
3. _____   8. _____
4. _____   9. _____
5. _____   10. _____

Jobs that people over 65 should *not* be allowed to do

1. _____   6. _____
2. _____   7. _____
3. _____   8. _____
4. _____   9. _____
5. _____   10. _____

1. At what age do most people retire in your country?
2. What do most people in your country do when they retire?
3. Are there any jobs that people in your country can't do after a certain age? What are they?

GAME Gossip

 TEAM | **GAME**

team number

At the retirement party, Alice Goodman and Mrs. Mendoza gossip about Rebecca. To **gossip** means to talk about someone when he/she can't hear you. Sometimes gossip is true, and sometimes it's false. Can you always tell the difference? Play this game and find out.

So, what do you think?

Very attractive, but a little too skinny.

Get Ready to Play

Step One
Work by yourself. Cut a piece of paper in half. Write "True" on one piece of paper and "Gossip" on the other piece. These will be your **True** and **Gossip** cards.

Step Two
Turn both sheets of paper over. On the back of your **True** card, write something about yourself that is true. Try to choose a true statement about yourself that no one else in the class knows. For example, maybe you like to play tennis, but no one in your class knows that about you. Here is how you would write your true statement.

EXAMPLE

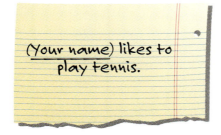

Step Three
On the back of your **Gossip** card, write something about yourself that isn't true. It's a good idea to try to choose something that might be true, but isn't. For example, maybe you hate to sing, but no one in your class knows that. In that case, your gossip card might look like this:

EXAMPLE

Step Four
Your teacher will help you with your cards. After everyone in the class has finished, give your **True** and **Gossip** cards to your teacher. Now you're ready to play!

EPISODE 23   PAGE 5

GAME Gossip

9	TEAM	GAME	

team number

Play the Game

- Divide into teams.
- Your teacher (or a class volunteer) will mix all the cards together and read them out loud.
- You and your teammates must decide whether the statement is **True** or **Gossip**. Check your answers in the scorecard below.
- After you've marked your team's choice in your scorecard, the person who wrote the question will say whether the statement is **True** or **Gossip**. If your team guessed correctly, put a (✔) in the score column.
- The team with the most correct answers wins the game.
- Use the scorecard below to play the game twice. You may need to write more **True** and **Gossip** cards.

SCORECARD

Game 1

Statement	True	Gossip	Score column	Statement	True	Gossip	Score column
1				17			
2				18			
3				19			
4				20			
5				21			
6				22			
7				23			
8				24			
9				25			
10				26			
11				27			
12				28			
13				29			
14				30			
15				31			
16							TOTAL POINTS

Game 2

Statement	True	Gossip	Score column	Statement	True	Gossip	Score column
1				17			
2				18			
3				19			
4				20			
5				21			
6				22			
7				23			
8				24			
9				25			
10				26			
11				27			
12				28			
13				29			
14				30			
15				31			
16							TOTAL POINTS

1. Do you think it's OK to gossip? Why or why not?
2. Do you ever gossip about other people?
3. How do you feel when other people gossip about you?

EPISODE 23   PAGE 6

The Phone Call

EPISODE 24

THEMES
- Parties
- Cheer Up!
- Bad News

GAME
- Making a Toast

OPTIONAL PROJECT
- Dancing (Appendix 12)

THEME Parties

1 GROUP SURVEY

_____
group number

People like to do many different things at parties. What do you like to do?

A. Rank the following activities from 1–5, with 1 as your favorite activity.

_____ dance   _____ talk to friends   _____ play games

_____ eat special food   _____ listen to music

B. Form groups of six to eight people. Try to have an equal number of men and women. Compare answers with your group. Write their answers in the chart below.

		What do you like to do at parties?				
Name	Sex (m/f)	Dance	Play games	Listen to music	Talk to friends	Eat special food

C. What's your group's favorite party activity? What's the least favorite?

D. Do women like different activities than men? What are the differences?

2 TEAM GAME   Time: 10 min.

_____
team number

What other things do you like to do at parties? With your team, make a list of all the things you can do at parties. Use your own paper. The team with the most activities wins.

3 PARTNER GAME

_____
partner's name

If you could invite one famous person to your party, who would you invite?

A. On a separate piece of paper, write the name of the famous person you would invite to your party. Don't let your partner see your paper!

B. Your partner will ask questions about your famous person and try to guess who it is. Your partner should ask you questions that only have *yes* or *no* for answers. Tell your partner the answer if he/she hasn't guessed it after 20 questions.

C. Take turns. Now you will ask your partner questions about his/her famous person.

THEME Cheer Up!

4 CLASS BRAINSTORM

I've got a little surprise to cheer you up.

In this episode, Alex is sad because he might have to move to Los Angeles. To **cheer up** her friend, Rebecca gives Alex a present.

To **cheer up** a friend means to say or do something that makes a friend feel better. As a class, think of different ways to cheer up a friend. Write your answers below.

1. Give him/her a present.
2. _____
3. _____
4. _____
5. _____
6. _____
7. _____
8. _____
9. _____
10. _____

EPISODE **24** PAGE **2**

5 GROUP INTERVIEW

group number

What do you do when you're sad? Do you ever cheer yourself up?
A. Form groups of four people.
B. Write your answers in the chart below.
C. Interview the people in your group. Ask the question: *When you are sad, how do you cheer yourself up?*
D. Write your group members' answers in the chart. Did any of their answers surprise you?

When you are sad, how do you cheer yourself up?			
You	Group member 1	Group member 2	Group member 3
go shopping	exercise	eat ice cream	talk to my best friend
1.	1.	1.	1.
2.	2.	2.	2.
3.	3.	3.	3.
4.	4.	4.	4.

6 PARTNER GREETING CARD

partner's name

In the United States and Canada, greeting cards are very popular. People often give greeting cards to cheer each other up.
A. Make a greeting card. Fold a piece of paper in half. Draw a picture on the front of the card.
B. Decide on a message to write inside the card.
C. When you finish, share your card with the class. If you want to, put your card in an envelope and mail it to a friend who you want to cheer up!

1. Have you ever cheered anyone up when he/she was sad?
2. If yes, what did you do?
3. If no, has anyone ever cheered you up when you were sad?

Episode 24   Page 3

THEME Bad News

1   PARTNER   WAYS TO SAY IT

_____
partner's name

In this episode, Rebecca gets some bad news about her father. It's difficult to give bad news in any language. To make it easier, people in the United States and Canada sometimes try to soften bad news by telling good news, too.

Work with a partner. Look at the situations below. Take turns practicing how to give both bad and good news. Then, make up your own situations.

Situations   **Expressions**

EXAMPLE   Your brother had a car accident. He isn't hurt.   I have some bad news and some good news. The bad news is that my brother had a car accident. The good news is that he isn't hurt.

1. You failed your math test. Your teacher will let you take the test again. Tell your parents.

2. You just broke up with your girlfriend/boyfriend. You agreed to stay friends. Tell your best friend.

3. You just lost your job. Your boss told you about a better job at a different company. Tell your husband/wife.

4. Your TV is broken. The store is having a sale. Tell your roommate.

5. Your sister is in the hospital. She's going to be OK. Tell your mother.

6. Your situation:

1. How do people give bad news in your country?
2. How do people react to bad news?
3. Have you ever given someone bad news? If so, what did you say?

EPISODE **24**   PAGE **4**

GAME Making a Toast

8 GROUP GAME

In this episode, Ramón and Alberto make special speeches in honor of their parents. These speeches are called toasts. In the United States and Canada, people make **toasts** at special celebrations.

Play this game, and practice making your own toasts.

Get Ready to Play

Step One
Divide into groups of four to six people. In your group, make a list of situations when people might make toasts. Write your answers below.

_____   _____
_____   _____
_____   _____
_____   _____
_____   _____

Step Two
Your teacher will check your list of situations to make sure they are all events where toasts can be made.

Step Three
Cut out the die and marker on Appendix 13. Write your initials on your marker.

Step Four
Choose one player's game board (page 6) as the official game board. You can cut it out of his/her book if you want to. Pass the game board to each player. Each player should write his/her first name on 10 of the empty squares on the game board. Only one name should be written on any square. Make sure all of the squares are filled. Add names to any empty squares. You are now ready to play the game. Follow the rules and have fun!

Play the Game
- Each player puts his/her marker on the gameboard at **GO**.
- Decide who goes first. Each player rolls the die. The player who rolls the highest number goes first, and play continues to the right.
- The first player rolls the die and moves his/her marker the number of spaces indicated (if a 2 is rolled, the marker is moved two spaces, and so on).
- If the player lands on a square with an opponent's name written on it, the opponent will choose a situation from the list on page 5. The player must then make a toast for that situation. The other players judge whether or not it is a good toast. If they decide it's a good toast, the player gets another turn. If they decide it's not a good toast, the player loses his/her turn, and the next person rolls the die.
- If the player lands on his/her own square, he/she loses a turn.
- The first player to reach the **STOP** square wins the game.

GAME Making a Toast

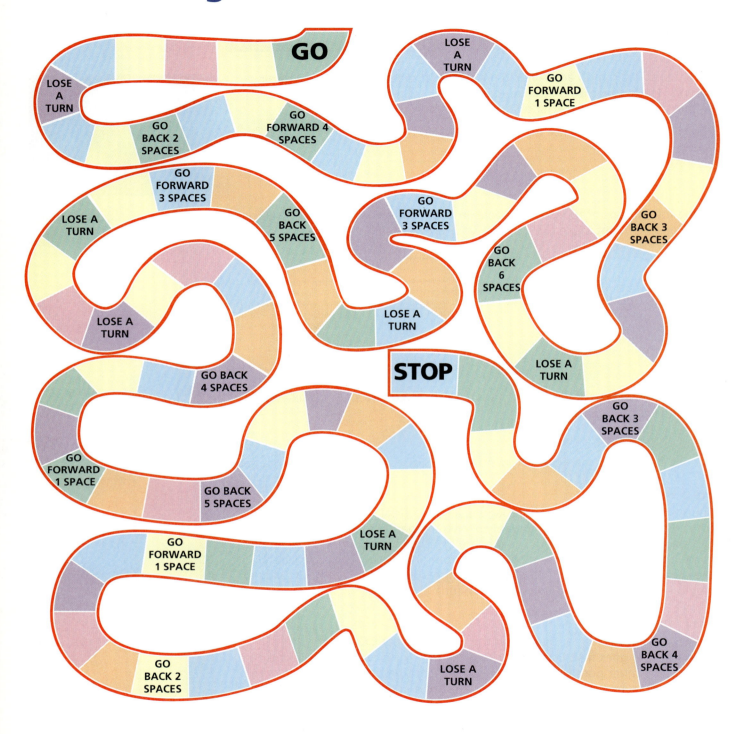

HOW TO DECIDE IF A TOAST IS GOOD

1. Does it begin with a good introduction?
   • "I'd like to propose a toast…"
   • "Here's to _____…"
   • "Let's toast _____…"

2. Does it give a reason for the toast?
   • A good toast should tell who (or what) the toast is about and why the toast is being made.

3. Does the toast make you laugh or cry?
   • Good toasts are often funny or sincere.

Episode 24   Page 6

EPISODE 13

PROJECT Culture Shock

 PARTNER **RESEARCH**

partner's name

At Rebecca's first dinner in San Francisco, Edward says to her, "You must be experiencing a certain amount of culture shock. . . moving to a new city, sharing this old house with people you don't know. . ." **Culture shock** is a feeling of nervousness or anxiety that people have when they are in a new place or a new culture. Have you ever experienced culture shock?

A. Work with a partner. Choose a city or a country that interests you both. It can be anywhere in the world, but it should be a place that neither of you has visited.

B. Find out as much as you can about this place. Use the Internet, encyclopedias, atlases, almanacs, or reference books for information.

C. If you go to this place, what would be different or unusual for you? Write down what you find out in the spaces below.

We would like to visit _____ .

These are some things that would be very different:

food

weather

customs

housing

holidays and festivals

other

 GROUP **DISCUSSION**

group number

Compare your list with that of another pair of students from your class. Ask them these questions:
- *What's most interesting about the place you want to visit?*
- *What would you like the most about living there?*
- *What do you think is the biggest difference between this place and where you live now?*

APPENDIX **1** EPISODE **13** PROJECT

EPISODE **14**

PROJECT **Looking for a Job**

1   **PARTNER**   **RESEARCH**

_____
partner's name

Work with a partner. Get a newspaper. Find the employment section of the classified ads. Look for ads for the jobs listed below. Check (✔) the ones you find.

_____ accountant	_____ electrician	_____ nurse
_____ artist	_____ engineer	_____ receptionist
_____ bank teller	_____ farm worker	_____ salesperson
_____ chef	_____ librarian	_____ social worker
_____ computer programmer	_____ manager	_____ tutor
	_____ model	_____ waiter
_____ dishwasher		

2   **GROUP**   **INTERVIEW**

_____
group number

A. Divide into groups. Each member of the group will find three people to interview outside of class. Ask this question: _What is your job now?_ Write the answer in the chart.
B. Then ask this question: _How did you find your job?_ Read the choices in the chart below.
C. Check (✔) their answers on the chart. If their answer is not in the chart, write it in under "Other."
D. Compare your information with that of the other people in your group. What is the most common way to find a job?

	The job	Classified ads in the newspaper	An employment agency	The employer's personnel office	People you know	Other
EXAMPLE	cake baker and decorator					✔ I opened my own business.

APPENDIX **2**   EPISODE **14** PROJECT

EPISODE 15

PROJECT Tourist Attractions

1 GROUP   RESEARCH

_____
group number

Divide into groups. Some tourists are visiting the place where you live for one day. You must write a complete schedule for their visit. Choose some popular tourist attractions in your area. Include them in the chart below. Get information from tourism books, phone books, newspapers, and so on. You can also call or visit people who work at local parks, restaurants, tourist attractions, and tourist agencies.

TOUR SCHEDULE

	Place/s	What you will do/eat there	Cost per person
Breakfast			
9 am–12 noon			
Lunch			
2 pm–5 pm			
Dinner			
Evening			

2 CLASS   DISCUSSION

As a class, compare each groups' schedule from Activity 1. On the board, make a list of the most popular places to visit. Combine these places into one "master" schedule. Make copies of the schedule and send it to local tourist agencies, chambers of commerce, and hotels. Be sure to send a letter with the schedule. In the letter, explain your class's project.

1. Do you usually use a guidebook when you visit tourist attractions?
2. Have you ever shown a tourist the city where you live?
3. Do you prefer to be the tourist or the host?
4. What is your favorite tourist attraction in your city?

EPISODE 16

PROJECT Working with Children

1 GROUP RESEARCH

_____
group number

In this episode, Rebecca has a job interview at an after-school program. After-school programs are very common in the United States and Canada. Children go to after-school programs until their parents are finished with work.

A. Look for information about a program in your area that's for children. It can be a weekend program, a summer program, or a daily program like the one in this episode. Use a telephone book, a local newspaper, or the Internet.
B. On the lines below, make a list of programs that you find.
C. Share your list with the rest of the class. Your teacher will write all the programs on a "master list" on the board.

1. _____
2. _____
3. _____
4. _____
5. _____

2 PARTNER RESEARCH

_____
partner's name

Work with a partner. Your teacher will assign you one of the programs from the list in Activity 1.

A. Find the answers to these questions. Get a brochure or a catalog from the program. Call on the telephone and interview someone who works there. Visit the program if you can. Write the information on a separate piece of paper.

1. What's the name of the program?
2. Where is the program?
3. What are the activities?
4. What hours is the program open?
5. How old are the children in the program?
6. Does the program cost anything? How much?
7. Are there any special rules or requirements for this program? What are they?
8. What other interesting information did you learn about this program?

B. Present your information to the class. Make a brochure or a handout with a list of important facts and information for everyone to have. Answer any questions that your classmates have. Talk about which programs are the most interesting.

APPENDIX 4   EPISODE 16 PROJECT

EPISODE 17

PROJECT Poetry

PARTNER RESEARCH

_____
partner's name

Do you read poetry? Have you ever read a poem by an American poet?

A. Work with a partner. Your teacher will assign you one of the following American poets.

Ogden Nash	Nikki Giovanni	Dr. Seuss	Sandra Cisneros
Robert Frost	Carl Sandburg	Edgar Allan Poe	Emily Dickinson
Henry Wadsworth Longfellow	Joyce Kilmer	Sylvia Plath	Maya Angelou

B. Go to your local or school library. Find a poem written by that poet.

C. Copy the poem on a clean sheet of paper. If it is a very long poem, copy only part of it.

D. Find out the answers to the following questions about the poet and the poem.

   1. What is the title of the poem? _____
   2. When was the poem written? _____
   3. Is the poet still alive? If not, when did the poet die? _____
   4. Where does/did the poet live? _____
   5. What do you think the poem is about? _____
   _____
   _____

   6. How does the poem make you feel? _____
   _____

   7. Do you have a favorite line from the poem? What is it? _____
   _____

PARTNER PRESENTATION

_____
partner's name

With your partner, make a presentation about your poem to the class.

A. Copy the poem onto a large piece of paper so the class can see it clearly.

B. Read the poem aloud to your classmates.

C. Tell about the poem and the poet. Use the answers to the questions in Activity 1, and add any other information that you have.

D. If you can, answer any questions that your classmates have about the poem.

EPISODE 18

PROJECT Going to an Art Gallery

group number

A. Use a local telephone book, newspaper, or magazine to make a list of five art galleries in your town or city, or a city nearby.
B. Discuss the names of the art galleries. Do any of the names tell you what kind of art the gallery has?

Name of art gallery	Address and telephone number
1.	
2.	
3.	
4.	
5.	

group number

A. In your groups, choose one of the galleries from your list in Activity 1.
B. Call the gallery and request a brochure or a catalog. If you can visit the gallery, interview someone who works there.
C. Find out the answers to these questions. Add one question of your own. Write your answers on a separate piece of paper.

  1. What kind of art does the gallery show?
  2. Does the gallery sell art, or just show it?
  3. If the gallery sells art, what is the price range of the art sold there?
  4. How often do the exhibits change?
  5. How many people visit the gallery each day?
  6. When is the busiest time of the week for the gallery?
  7. How is the art chosen?
  8. Your question:

D. In your group, work together to write a summary of the information about your art gallery. Post your summary on a wall or bulletin board in your school where other students can read about the gallery. Decorate the bulletin board with any brochures or photographs about the gallery that you have collected.

1. Have you ever visited an art gallery?
2. Have you ever been to a gallery opening?
3. If you could, what kind of art would you buy? Why?

APPENDIX 6 EPISODE 18 PROJECT

EPISODE 19

PROJECT Team Games

1 GROUP RESEARCH

group number

In the United States and Canada, the following team games are popular:

football

volleyball

ice hockey

basketball

Divide into groups. Each group chooses a different team game from above. Complete the information below about your game. Use a separate piece of paper. Use your school or public library, an encyclopedia, the Internet, and so on. Try to find pictures of your game.

Name of game _____

1. How many players are on a team?
2. Where is the game played (*on a field, on a court, and so on*)?
3. What special equipment is needed to play the game?
4. What actions (skills) are used to play the game? Write as many *action verbs* as you can—for example, *run, kick*, and so on.
5. How do you score points in the game?
6. Is there a time limit to the game? If yes, how much time does it take to play a game?
7. What is one new thing you learned about this game?

2 GROUP POSTER

group number

A. On a large sheet of paper, make a poster for your team game. Be sure to do the following:
   ■ Write the name of your game at the top of your poster in large letters.
   ■ Write a paragraph that tells about your game.
   ■ Draw or paste pictures of your game next to the paragraph.
B. Present your poster to the class. Hang up your posters so your classmates can look at them. Vote on the best poster.

1. What's your favorite team game? Do you like to play this game or watch it?
2. Who's your favorite athlete or sports hero? Why?
3. What team game is most popular in your home country?

EPISODE 20

PROJECT Greeting Cards

1 · PARTNER · RESEARCH

partner's name

In this episode, the children at the after-school program make homemade greeting cards for Vincent. What kinds of cards can you buy? Where can you buy them?

A. Work with a partner. Call or visit a store that sells greeting cards. Check (✔) the kinds of greeting cards that the store sells.

_____ birthday cards
_____ cards that say "Congratulations"
_____ anniversary cards
_____ blank cards (no message inside)
_____ graduation cards
_____ sympathy cards
_____ friendship cards
_____ cards that say "I love you"
_____ religious cards
_____ cards especially for family members
_____ thank you cards
_____ get well cards

B. Find out the answers to the questions below.

1. What kind of card does the store sell the most of? _____
2. Does the store have other cards that aren't on the list? _____
3. What are the names of some of the companies that make greeting cards? _____

2 · GROUP · SURVEY

group number

When do you send a card?

A. Read the questions in the chart below and check (✔) your answers.
B. Interview three people outside your class. Ask the question: *Do you sometimes send a card to tell someone you're sorry?* Check their answers.
C. Compare your survey answers with those of your group. What is the most common reason to send a card?

Do you sometimes send a card...	You	Person 1	Person 2	Person 3
1. to tell someone you're sorry?				
2. to wish someone a happy birthday?				
3. to say thank you?				
4. to say hello to a friend?				
5. to express sympathy when someone has died?				
6. (other)				

1. When do you receive cards?
2. Who sends you cards?
3. What kind of cards do you like to receive?
4. What do you do with the cards you receive?

APPENDIX 8   EPISODE 20 PROJECT

EPISODE 21

PROJECT Making Decisions

1 GROUP SURVEY

_____
group number

In this episode, the Wangs have to make a difficult decision about Vincent and the after-school program. Interview three people outside of your class to find out how they feel about making difficult decisions.

Step One
Introduce your survey like this:
I'm doing a survey. It's about making difficult decisions. Would you answer some questions?

Step Two
Start the survey like this:
Please answer *Yes* or *No* to the first six questions I ask you.

Step Three
Write the answers to the questions in the chart below. For numbers 1-6, check (✔) the answer. For number 7, write the answer.

Have you ever made a difficult decision about. . .	Person 1		Person 2		Person 3	
	Yes	No	Yes	No	Yes	No
1. where you and your family should live?	❑	❑	❑	❑	❑	❑
2. whether or not to spend a large amount of money?	❑	❑	❑	❑	❑	❑
3. who to marry or divorce?	❑	❑	❑	❑	❑	❑
4. whether or not to quit a job?	❑	❑	❑	❑	❑	❑
5. how to discipline a child?	❑	❑	❑	❑	❑	❑
6. a situation that would hurt another person's feelings?	❑	❑	❑	❑	❑	❑
7. What was the hardest decision you ever had to make?						

2 GROUP DATA ANALYSIS

_____
group number

Divide into groups. Compare surveys with the people in your group.

A. Answer these questions:

- Is there a question that everyone answered "Yes" to? Which one? _____

- Is there a question that everyone answered "No" to? Which one? _____
  Discuss these results with your group.

B. With your group, categorize the answers from question 7. Count the number of decisions that have to do with money, family, health, children, and so on. What kind of decision is most often mentioned?

APPENDIX **9** EPISODE **21** PROJECT

EPISODE 22

PROJECT Television

| 1 | GROUP | SURVEY |

group number

Television is a very popular leisure activity in the United States and Canada. Complete this survey to find out how the people you know feel about television.

A. Divide into groups. Read the questions in the chart below. What do you think most people will say? Predict which answers will be *the most common*, and circle them in the Prediction column.

B. Find three people from outside your class and interview them about their television habits. Read them the questions and answers in the chart below, and circle their answers.

Alex, turn off that television this minute!

	Prediction	Person 1	Person 1	Person 1
1. Do you enjoy watching television?	Yes No	Yes No	Yes No	Yes No
2. How many televisions do you have in your house?	1 2 3 more than 3	1 2 3 more than 3	1 2 3 more than 3	1 2 3 more than 3
3. How many hours a day do you watch television?	1-2 2-3 more than 3 other _____	1-2 2-3 more than 3 other _____	1-2 2-3 more than 3 other _____	1-2 2-3 more than 3 other _____
4. When do you usually watch television?	morning afternoon evening late at night	morning afternoon evening late at night	morning afternoon evening late at night	morning afternoon evening late at night
5. What kind of television shows do you prefer to watch?	comedies drama documentaries news other _____	comedies drama documentaries news other _____	comedies drama documentaries news other _____	comedies drama documentaries news other _____

C. Meet with your group again. How many of your predictions were accurate?

1. What is your favorite television program?
2. Why do you like it?
3. How many hours a week do you spend watching television?
4. Do you think television has a positive or negative effect on children? Explain your answer.

EPISODE 23

PROJECT International Celebrations

group number

In this episode, Mr. and Mrs. Mendoza celebrate their retirement with many of the same customs found in a typical Mexican fiesta. For example, there is Mexican music, food, and dancing.

A. Look at the chart below. In groups, decide on one event and one country. Circle them. If you want to, you can choose an event or country that is not on the list.

Event	Country
wedding	Greece
birth of a child	Japan
anniversary	Australia
new job	Nigeria
retirement	Argentina
other event	other country

B. Find out how people celebrate the event that you chose in the country you circled. You can interview a friend or classmate, or use your school library, magazines, the Internet, and so on. Write your answers on a separate piece of paper.
  1. What is the event?
  2. What is the country?
  3. Are there any special foods at the celebration? What are they?
  4. Are there special gifts at the celebration? What kind?
  5. Are there other special things that happen at the celebration, such as dancing, music, or special decorations? What are they?

C. Share your information with your classmates. If you want, your group can create a poster about your celebration for the rest of the class to enjoy.

Now that you have learned about many different parties from around the world, it's time to throw an international celebration of your own.

A. Choose one of the reports on celebrations in different countries from Activity 1.
B. Divide into groups. Each group should be in charge of one of the following things: food, music, gifts, decorations, and other special customs.
C. Pick a date for your party and have fun!

EPISODE 24

PROJECT Dancing

1 PARTNER RESEARCH

partner's name

People often dance at parties. In this episode, people dance at the retirement party for Mr. and Mrs. Mendoza.

A. Work in pairs. Find out about dances in other countries. Use your library, an encyclopedia, the Internet, and so on.

B. Each pair chooses a different country. Find out about one type of dancing in that country. Write your information below.

Country _____

Name of dance _____

Description of the dance _____

_____

_____

Where do people usually see or do this kind of dance? _____

_____

2 PARTNER POSTER

partner's name

With your partner from Activity 1, make a poster about your dance.
- Include a photograph or drawing of the dance.
- Include a written description of the dance.
- Present your poster to the class. Your teacher may want to hang it on the wall.

1. What kinds of dancing do you like?
2. Do you go dancing a lot?
3. What dances are popular in your country?
4. Can you do these dances?

APPENDIX 12   EPISODE 24 PROJECT

APPENDIX 13 Manipulatives

Episode 14

Episode 18

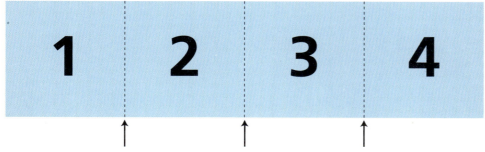

Cut out die. Fold here and tape together.

Episode 24

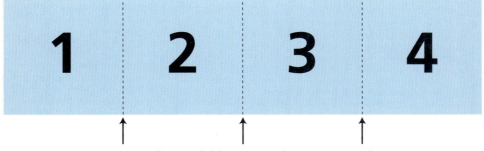

Cut out die. Fold here and tape together.

◯ Write your initials on this marker.